The Will

of

Annie

By Anthony GIBLIN

i

Cover Illustration by Annie Giblin

Copyright © Anthony Giblin, 2021

In Memory of Annie Giblin

1942 - 1981

Table of Contents

THE WILL

OF

ANNIE

Prologue

I would presume there's not a man in the world who has not experienced the pain from the impact of something colliding with his balls at some stage or other. I would presume again they have never forgotten the first collision, be it a fall or a ball, a kick or a stick. It is an agonising revelation as to the most sensitive part of the male body.

My revelation came during the summer break from school at seven years of age. It was a fine day in Shard End Park, near my home, where I played with my sister Tracey and friends in a maze, made from upright logs five foot high and cast in concrete footings. I was lost and panicking as I ran from cul de sac to cul de sac, so I decided to climb onto the top of the logs and walk along the green mossy tops where I could see everyone else running up and down the dead ends of the maze. I could also see a way out. In the excitement of freedom I started to run, lost my balance and came down fast with a leg either side of a log top.

For a moment I felt no pain at all and began to lift myself up again. Then it came. It came so strong that I just slid to my right and landed on the ground in silence and out of breath, clutching my balls and rolling myself over and over on the gravel floor till my breath came back. With that, came my voice and I sang, using the song to compliment my dance.

Later, at home and in no pain at all, I took a wee in the toilet and thought of all the strange looks on the people's faces as I sprinted through our council estate, still singing and still clutching. Then, I noticed my entire scrotum was purple. I called my mother who was all the good things a mother can be, and she was mine, well not just mine. I shared her with my older brother and four sisters, but this didn't seem to moderate the mothering I received.

"Mommy, mommy, come here quick. Quick mom. There's something wrong."
She responded to my cry for help immediately.

"What's all the shouting about, Anthony?" she asked as she held the toilet door open.

"Look mom," I said as I leaned back against the wall of the small toilet with my trousers down holding my small willy to one side.

"Oh Jesus, Mary and Joseph, Anthony are you in pain loveen?"

"No, not anymore."

"We have to get you to a doctor."

At the doctor's there was a queue of eight people but mom led me by the hand over to reception and spoke to Nurse Harrison, a curly haired, fellow Irish woman who led us straight into her surgery room.

"Anthony, show nurse Harrison, good boy."

So, I pulled down my elasticated polyester trousers and under pants and held my little willy to the side and arched my back as I looked up to see nurse Harrison's reaction. She was blessing herself.

"Oh, good God, are you in pain child? Pull up your trousers quick, you're going up to see Doctor Cranston," she said.

"He told me earlier he's *not* in pain," Mom said as I tucked myself in.

"Bring him up, Annie, right away, I'll talk to the doctor."

"Hello, Annie, and who's this little fellah?" Doctor Cranston said as he looked over half rim glasses from behind his desk.

"This is Anthony, he's the second youngest. He fell earlier today doctor and hurt his privates."

"Oh, is he in pain? Are you in pain young man?"

"No," I replied.

"Anthony, show the doctor," Mom said.

The doctor didn't panic at the sight of my purple scrotum like mom and nurse Harrison did. But he *did* check if they were still there. I knew they were because I had done the same earlier once the pain went away.

"Well Annie, he's not in any pain and everything is where it should be, so I think he's just badly bruised. I see a few more bruises around his legs, which suggests he's a child who bruises quite easily so monitor him over the next few days and return him to me if there's anything out of the ordinary."

"Okay doctor, so that is it then?"

"That's it Annie. And Annie, you were right to bring him."

"Okay, thank you doctor."

CRUMLIN DUBLIN 2012

Monday, early evening, and the heat in the children's hospital is making me drowsy, being togged out for a construction site isn't helping. My alarm clock, as always, woke me at 5.30 am. My day on site was cut short around eight thirty when I got a call from my wife, Niamh, who was crying.

"Anthony, the doctors are wrong, I'm telling you. The doctors are wrong. Annie has just tripped again trying to rush to the toilet to vomit. I can't bring her to school today, it's time we did something different."

"Okay, okay, Niamh, I'm coming home. I'm going to bring her to the children's hospital myself, to put your mind at rest if nothing else."

So, I unbuckled my belt, of nail-bag and hammer, and slung it across the passenger seat. She suspects that there's something seriously wrong with our seven-year-old daughter Annie. She *has* done for a few months now.

"Google her symptoms," she stated last week.

"She's fine Niamh, she's just a clumsy child."

"Okay Ant, that's why she trips. What about her headaches, what about her vomiting?"

"Well, maybe the doctors are right, she wears glasses and maybe it's migraine."

"The doctors are wrong Anthony and I know it."

Niamh is a worrier and can panic at times, but yesterday I felt perhaps I should find out one way or the other, and that maybe I had my head in the sand. With Annie on the couch under a duvet, and our two younger boys playing in our backyard, in the early April sunshine, I googled her symptoms into my iPad. A lot came up, but brain tumour came up the most.

It's been a long day, with two different doctors doing tests on Annie. It started with physical tests of hand movements, walking in a straight line, balancing on one leg, then it was the CAT scan and now this MRI machine. But she seems content now, as she's able to watch Shrek in this one. With the lights off, my eyes are drawn to the large neon circle of the machine in which she lies, and the plugs they gave me are fully swelled in my ears. Taking the edge off the varying drones the machine is making. My head is heavy, my eyes are closing, one, then two.

The drop of my head wakes me up and I lift it and try to hold it, my gaze is level with the neon circle, and I watch it blur, as I go again. *There's a ship pulling out, its horn is blaring. I have to get on board. It's too late.*

"Mr Giblin. Mr Giblin."

I awaken and there's a nurse standing between me and the circle.

"What, oh sorry. I dozed off," I say as I wipe the dribble from my chin.

"Mr Giblin, could you follow me, please."

"Yes, of course."

I leave the dark room with Annie still in the machine. I follow the nurse through a room where the bright lights are stinging my eyes. *How long had I dozed*? The nurse leads me to another room on the left, where there are four people sitting down. They all rise as I enter and look at me. That's when I see one of them is my wife and that's when I know something is wrong. I feel my stomach tightening and swallow hard on nothing.

"Niamh, what are you doing here?"

"I couldn't wait around."

"Who's got the boys?"

"My mother."

Her mother! Her mother's driven over four hours to mind the boys, fuck! There is the heavy-set man who was testing Annie's balance earlier in the day. He has a round, friendly face. There is another nurse, I had met earlier, with long curly dark red hair and pale freckled skin. She could nearly pass for one of our own. But it is a small lady who steps forward and speaks. I've never seen her before, though she has a familiar look.

"Hello Anthony, I'm Katie Brennan, Head of the Neuro Oncology Department. This is Doctor Peter Kavanagh, and this is Nurse Marie Cassidy." *I don't want to be here, I want to go backwards to yesterday or the day before.*

I shake hands with all three of them as Katie instructs us all to sit. I sit beside Niamh and she pulls her chair closer. I look at her and wonder if I look as worried as she does.

"Now Niamh, Anthony," Katie says, "the CAT scan has revealed a tumour in the back of Annie's brain."

Niamh makes a noise in her throat. I look at her, our eyes meeting. I reach for her hand. Swallowing hard, I watch her eyes fill, then overflow as Katie is still talking. What she is saying now is secondary in my mind, I am far away... "You'll be taken to Temple Street Children's Hospital on the other side of town.

There will be a team there waiting for you." I hug Niamh, my head in her shoulder as she sobs into my neck. After a moment I pull back as I feel my mind clearing. "Okay. What's going to happen?" I ask, as I receive a box of tissues from Doctor Kavanagh.

"Can it be removed?" Niamh says, as she takes tissues.

"Yes, Niamh, and it will be. We need to get the results of this MRI scan and that won't be until morning. Then we send them over to Temple Street. On receiving them, they will take action, and by action, I mean they will operate."

Katie's words take me away from this moment. *My Annie. No. Oh no. Not an operation. A tumour on her brain. Oh please no.* I realise I'm mumbling my thoughts. Nurse Marie takes my left hand as Niamh takes my right and places her head into my shoulder with heavy sobs. I feel my mind clearing again and stand up, breaking all contact.

"Okay, we need to go," I say. They look up at me and Katie rises to her feet and places her hands on my upper arms.

"We need to go," I repeat.

"Anthony, did you drive here?" Katie asks.

"Yes."

"You can't drive now because you are not in the right frame of mind and anyway, Annie is our patient. We will get an ambulance to bring you over. If they are too busy, we will pay for a taxi and your car here won't be charged for parking."

Niamh stands up, then Peter and Marie rise to their feet. Katie takes her hands away and turns. "Niamh, there's a great doctor over in Temple Street. Doctor Mark Timmins. He's a Paediatric Neurosurgeon and he will be taking care of Annie."

"Okay."

"Is there any history of tumours in the family?" Katie says.

Niamh swallows hard as we exchange a glance.

"Yes, Katie. Anthony's mother died of a tumour on the brain in 1981."

"Well, things have come on a great deal since 1981. Marie, bring Annie out to her parents."

She is barely in the doorway holding Marie's hand when Niamh and I rush to her with hugs and kisses. Then, Katie leads us through the hospital corridors and down a stairwell onto the ground floor. As she walks with us, she places her hands onto our arms and backs like she's protecting us from everyone else. She strokes Annie's hair as she gives instructions to a passing nurse. Katie leads us to a bright room with windows on one side, and smiling, wide-eyed fish and bubbles painted on the other. She introduces us to a nurse called Helen.

"Helen here will look after you while I organise transportation to Temple Street." I sit beside Annie and turn her back to the doorway and hold her hand as I watch Niamh on the phone in the hallway breaking the news to her family. Tears flowing. Helen brings tea and toast on a tray and I realise I haven't eaten all day, so I pour some tea and open the small rectangles of butter packs with a knife. I cover my toast with butter while I ponder the problem of returning to collect my car.

I can drive now; my head is clear. I'll let Niamh and Annie go in the ambulance, otherwise I'll be stranded over the other side of town. My car could get stolen or clamped, at least if it gets clamped it wouldn't get stolen. I continue to spread the butter around the toast. I raise the toast to my mouth but I can't eat it, so I put it down and turn to Annie and she cuddles into my chest and yawns, and so do I. I watch Niamh standing in the hallway talking into her phone, a passing nurse hands her a tissue then goes on her busy way again. I drink the tea and wonder why I'm not so emotional. My thoughts return to the car again. *I don't really care about the damn car. I should call my family too.*

I know I have to call the family, but I don't want to break the news to Dad. I decide I'm going to call my sister Tracey and ask her to tell everyone else. Then I decide we'll go together, and I will get a taxi back when Niamh and Annie are settled in Temple Street. I touch the keys in my pocket and stroke Annie's hair.

On arrival at Temple Street Children's Hospital in Dublin, I hand the taxi driver the payment slip Katie Brennan had given me, but I hold the large brown envelope tight to my chest. "Now these are very important details Anthony," she'd observed, "It's the disc with the results of the CAT scan and you must hand them in immediately at the reception of the Neuro Oncology Department. Now Anthony, Niamh and Annie, God Bless you, I will see you again."

FOR THE IMMEDIATE ATTENTION OF DOCTOR TIMMINS

is written on the envelope. With my emotions numb and my head clear, we follow the hospital porter as he pushes Annie in a wheelchair through the warm, bright corridors, the walls decorated with animals, dinosaurs, and fish. We enter the lift and stand closely around the wheelchair as the doors close. The porter's pot-belly is straining the middle buttons of his white shirt. The back and sides are tucked down into his trousers but the front drapes from the navel. I feel the need to talk to him.

"I was told to hand this envelope in immediately, mate."

"Yeah, I'll show you where, Bud."

On the fourth floor of the Neuro Oncology Department, the porter hands the envelope to the receptionist, then two nurses take Annie to a bed, in a four-bed room, two on either side as we walk in and a long window straight in front. Annie's is on the right, nearest the window. Only two of the other beds have children in them, one boy sitting up with a heavily bandaged head as he scribbles on a pad, a slim, tired looking woman seated beside him. She smiles with a slight nod as our eyes meet. The other child, I can't tell if it's a boy or a girl, just a small body lies under a sheet with wires and tubes attached to bleeping machines. A man is seated beside the bed reading a book.

"And what's this pretty girl's name with the beautiful long hair?"

The pony-tailed nurse says as she helps Annie onto the bed.

Niamh and I stand back, smiling as we wait for Annie's reply, but she is fixing herself in the bed and doesn't respond.

"Well, my name is Mags and this is Lailani," she says introducing the smiling Filipino nurse beside her.

"My name is Annie."

"Oh Annie," Mags says, "that's a lovely name. Is it because of your red, curly hair?" Mags looks at Niamh.

"No," Niamh attempts a smile. "We named her Annie after Anthony's mother."

"It's auburn," Annie corrects.

"Oh, I'm sorry, it *is* auburn Annie, and a beautiful auburn it is too," Mags says as she winks at Niamh. Lailani slides two chairs over from under the window and I take them from her.

"Sit down and try to get comfortable," she says.

"Thank you."

"You're welcome," Lailani says with a hint of Irish in her accent.

Niamh and I sit in the chairs at the side of the bed, holding hands as Annie sits up eating sausages and chips, looking totally healthy and out of place in these surroundings. She seems to understand that she is here to make her headaches go away as Niamh explained it to her in the taxi. We sit for a while, not talking, listening to the sounds of the ward, the bleeps and grinds of the machines, the phones ringing in reception, the nurses talking, a distant child's voice. Niamh squeezes my hand tighter and I turn, and we search each other's eyes for a moment, I watch a tear build, then fall, slithering down her pale cheeks.

A man approaches.

"Hi, I'm Doctor Mark Timmins, you must be Annie's parents?"

Niamh and I stand straight away, our chairs screeching, to greet the doctor, a tall, slim, handsome man in full green surgery garb.

"Yes," I say, "I'm Anthony, this is Niamh."

"Hello, Doctor," Niamh says as we shake his hand.

The doctor looks at Annie, then back to us and says, …."Do you mind Anthony, Niamh, if we just have a quick word in the hallway?"

"No, go ahead," Niamh says, and we follow the doctor as he makes long strides towards the door.

"I viewed the disc of the Cat Scan and I'm awaiting the disc of the MRI but from what I see now, Annie has a posterior fossa mass, that's the tumour, situated in the middle to the rear of her head. Let me draw you a sketch."

"Yes, I'd prefer that" I say, as he reaches for an admission card and a pen from the reception desk nearby. He sketches an almost perfect side profile of a child's head and face, starting at the throat and finishing at the back of the neck.

"I will open the skull here and the tumour is here, superiorly within the cerebellum anterior. I will remove the tumour from an opening I will make here, stitch it back up, and we will deal with things from there. I won't have to cut much of Annie's beautiful hair. It will just be a strip that will hardly be noticed."

My heart is racing as I stand there, holding Niamh's hand, while trying to take in what he says. He smiles and says, "Do you have any questions?" "The opening...the...opening in the skull, will that heal itself or what happens?" I say, "Of course, Anthony. A child's skull will heal in no time but, as I said, I won't receive the MRI results till tomorrow, and I'll know more then.
But either way, we will be operating tomorrow, 1pm approximately."

"And how long does surgery take?" Niamh asks, stealing the question from my lips.

"Four, five hours," he looks at us. "It's been a tough day for you two, so we'll talk more tomorrow

11

morning," he says with a smile, before he turns and makes long strides down the corridor.

It's after seven in the evening when Annie realises, she has left Snowy in the car. "Daddy, please will you get him. I won't sleep without him," Snowy is Annie's 'chosen one' from the time she was a few weeks old, a soft, cuddly white mouse that was as big as her at the time of being chosen from the many cuddly toys bestowed upon our first born. Seven years on and machine washed numerous times from vomit, Snowy bears a slim resemblance to his former, full, furry self. But Annie is forever loyal, none the less.

"Of course, I will. I have to collect the car any way," I say, looking from Annie to Niamh.

"Will you be okay to drive Ant?"

"Yeah, I'm good for the drive. I'll get a taxi outside and I'll be back in an hour or two. Is there anything you need from a shop?"

"No, but I'll have a list for you to bring from home in the morning, only one parent can stay overnight and there's a pull-out mattress down there for a parent to sleep on. I'll be grand, Sure. See you in a bit."

"Okay," I say, as I touch the keys in my pocket and leave the room, selfishly pleased to be leaving this environment for a while.

I use the time to call my working partners Danny Doyle and Tommy Collins. We're a small company, DCG Construction, that started seven years earlier. We specialise in reinforced concrete structures and have been fortunate to remain busy throughout the downturn. I call Danny.

"Mother of fuck, a tumour. A tumour!" Danny says, then goes quiet.

"Are you there Danny? Danny?"

"I am," his tone lowers.

"When I know more, I'll talk to you but I won't be around for a few days."

"Giblin, don't worry about work for fuck sake. You have enough on your plate, but call me tomorrow, please, with any bit of news."

"Yes, I will Danny, talk then."

"Okay, good luck."

Danny's a big, tough, west of Ireland man, with vocals to match, which he uses to full effect on site, where he's a hard goer, with a quick brain. But concealed, on site, is the big soft heart of a good man.

I call Tommy.

"A tumour on the brain? And where is she now? When are they operating?"

"Temple Street, Tom. The operation is tomorrow as soon as they get the MRI results."

"Do you need us to look after the two boys? Josephine! Josephine! Come here, listen to this." I hold my answer as I hear Tommy briefing his wife.

"Anthony, Josephine here can go over to your place and look after the two boys."

"No, no. Niamh's mother Mary is back at the house with them and there's more of her family coming from Mayo in the morning.

"Okay Anthony, look after the family and keep us posted, won't you? God bless now."

"Thankyou. God bless you too."

On arriving back at Temple Street, I drive around the front of the hospital and the side roads, searching for a parking space. After ten minutes I give up and drive down a narrow lane between two of the hospital buildings. Slowly, I drive looking for a spot. Then I see a black car inappropriately parked. As I ease around it, I see two suited men carrying a white four-foot coffin into a side entrance. Around the corner I find a parking space, where I collect my emotions for a moment.

I walk to the front hospital entrance, the sky is darkening, but with a fringe of orange just over the roofs of the flats opposite. The security man in the bright reception area nods, I nod back, then head for a coffee machine before I make my way up to the Neuro Oncology Department to the familiar nurses, with their warm reassuring smiles. I turn into the ward; no lamps are on and the semi-darkness gives the room a stillness. Annie lies sleeping with Niamh rubbing her forehead down to her crown, over and over.

"You weren't too long," she whispers.

"No, just parking seems to be an issue around here," I say, lowering my tone as I hear myself. I place Snowy under Annie's arm and I smile at the reunion. I sit in the seat and siphon back the last drop of coffee through the lid-slot, and Niamh turns suddenly as the sharp echo of the cup fracturing a little, startles her. "You'll need to go soon. I have a list of things I want brought from home, try and be early in the morning. There's a counsellor or therapist lady who wants to speak to us. She was here. She's lovely Ant, and there's forms of consent we have to sign before they operate."

This quickens my heart again.

"Jesus, I won't be late," I say, as I rub my hand through my hair. "But I think I'll head home now, okay?"

"Okay, I love you".

"I love you too."

We hug, but I keep it brief.

"Bye Ant."

"Bye."

It saddens me leaving Annie and Niamh behind. It's a lonesome drive home. *I have to be strong. I have to be strong for my family.* It's black-dark when I pull up to the drive of our house, and though the days this past week have been fine and dry, the nights are a chilly reminder of the time of year. I rush to my door, and in the dining room I'm met by the great warmth of a real fire. Niamh's mother, Mary, puts a fire down in her own house in Mayo, every day of the year, with their own cut turf from the bog. And does so in our house, (with their own cut turf), on every visit. She rises from the chair beside the fire when I enter the room, a small sturdy woman, her dark hair disarranged and eyes heavily swollen. We don't speak, as she puts her arms around me, and I can't hold back. I cry, a heavy cry over her shoulder. Eventually I croak out the words.

"Are the boys in bed?"

"They are, I put Luke down with a bottle an hour ago. And Mikey's only gone ten minutes. He was shattered the cretchur, he was asking for Annie. I told him the doctors are making her headaches go away and that she needs her mother beside her for a few days. I was talking to Niamh on the phone, they're operating tomorrow."

"Yeah."

"Oh God help us and save us. The phone here hasn't stopped."

"I can imagine."

"Half of Mayo must be lit with candles for her, God love her. I have dinner for you, you must be starved."

"I'd eat a bite."

With my dinner, I pour myself a sizeable amount of red wine and there are no leftovers. Mary is talking about John, Niamh's father, how she had to leave without him as he was at work. But he is on his way with Niamh's sister Rachel and husband Steve. She tells me that my father called from Birmingham and he and my sister Tracey are arranging flights to come over. "Thank you, Mary," I say as I retreat to my bed.

I lie down to sleep, I can't. My body wants rest, but my mind is racing. I turn to my side and the sound of the MRI machine is in my head. I lie on my back and I see hospital corridors. There are too many pillows, that's what the problem is. I shove them all away except one and lie on my back with my hands behind my head. *If I leave my eyes open, they might close by themselves.* I try but they don't. *Niamh isn't here beside me; Annie's bed is empty. What made this happen? What am I at fault for? Am I some sort of toy to a warped God? A God who makes a boy, makes him a nice boy, soft heart, sensitive even, born to a loving mother and father, then takes the mother away when he's nine. Just when he's got used to her, He takes her away, a tumour on the brain. Then further on, when he finds happiness again in fatherhood, his first born that he calls after his mother...a tumour on the brain. Is this a test? I feel like a little pig in a fairy tale where god is the big bad wolf with such great lungs.*

In the morning I wake, look around my familiar bedroom ceiling. I smile with relief that everything is a nightmare. Then I turn over to Niamh. She isn't here, I sit up, my mind comes to focus and all of yesterday comes back as my heart stalls a beat, followed by rapid beats to amend, and a sick feeling in my stomach. I think of Annie and Niamh waking in the busy ward and I feel shit, guilt for having my own bed in peace. *I need a shave, I'd better get moving.* I remember my thoughts of last night. *I was wrong, those thoughts were wrong. What made me think like that. That was bullshit. I should never feel sorry for myself, my poor brother and sisters all suffered. And Dad. And it's Annie that's sick. I believe God is good. I need to be strong. I need to get moving.*

With everything on Niamh's list packed into two bags, I drive out of North Kildare and into Dublin as the spell of good weather continues. In the city, I scour Temple Street for parking, eventually slotting into a spot just as it becomes vacant. The hospital seems an awful lot busier this morning, with staff coming and going, immersed in their own work. All four of the beds in the ward Annie shares are now occupied. A small girl with a swollen head being the new arrival. Niamh and Annie are pleased to see me.

"Daddy, thank you. I woke up this morning with Snowy."

"Ahh, you're welcome, Annie," I say, as I lean over to kiss her.

"Did you sleep okay?"

"Yes Daddy."

"How about you, Niamh?"

"Not much. An hour here and an hour there. It's so noisy with the machines whirring and bleeping and the phones ringing out in the hallway. Anyway, did you bring me everything on the list?"

"I think so."

"Great. There's a parent bathroom with shower down the hallway. Pass me the bags."

I sit at Annie's bedside while Niamh freshens up and makes a trip to the canteen. When she returns, she starts telling me about some of the parents she has spoken to.

"That girl in the bed in the corner. Don't look," she whispers. "She's been here nearly two months now. She fell and banged her head. Now she has to learn everything she was taught in her four years all over again. Her mother and father split their time between here and looking after their eighteen-month old twins at home. The girl's name is Ali, Eileen is her mother."

"Jesus," I say, shaking my head.

"Anthony, we could be here for a long time too, depending on the outcome."

"We'll go one day at a time Niamh."

"I know. I know."

Doctor Mark Timmons approaches us at the bedside in formal clothes, black trousers, and white shirt, which makes him look younger than the day before.

"Good morning Niamh, Anthony. Do you mind if we have a quick word?"

"No problem," I say as I stand up.

"Annie, we'll just be out in the hallway for a minute," Niamh says.

We follow the doctor out of the ward into the hallway where he stops in front of the reception desk.

"Okay, I have slightly better news this morning."

"That's good," I say, as Niamh squeezes my hand.

"The MRI results have shown things a little differently, more accurately, they always do. They have shown me the tumour is smaller than first suspected. It's measuring 5.3 cm x 6.8cm which is still a large tumour especially in a child's head but it's still smaller than first suspected and most importantly, it's a little lower than we thought. So, I will be going in and removing it from a more natural opening, lower in the skull, which is an improvement on last night."

"Okay doctor and what time will she be going down for surgery?" Niamh says.

"The nurse will start preparing her at 1pm so she will be brought down to the theatre at 1.30 and you can walk with her as far as the doors with T1 on them. Okay? Is there anything else?"

"No...no doctor...thank you doctor," I say as I put my hand out. He looks at me and shakes it, he puts his other one on my shoulder and says,

"Look, I've performed this surgery over sixty times now and though I can't make any guarantees, no patient has died as a result of the surgery. I've had unavoidable complications but no deaths.

After surgery, we have to send the tumour over to the Lab to be tested and that can take up to a week. So, we will just take one hurdle at a time."

He smiles as he takes his hand from my shoulder and I let go of his.

"Thanks again doctor," Niamh says, wiping her eyes and smiling.

We sit beside Annie's bed holding hands but not talking, both lost in our thoughts. I notice Annie looking at the two of us, so I straighten myself in the chair and say, "Niamh, I feel a lot better after that chat with the doctor. Annie in two hours you're going down to a room where you're going to sleep, and the doctor is going to give you medicine to take the bad pain away from your head. He's going to make you better."

"Will it hurt Daddy?"

"No, he said you won't feel a thing because you will be fast asleep, and you'll wake up better."

"But all the other children look hurt!"

Niamh senses my struggle and adds, "Annie, all those children are healing. They were very sick, but they are getting better so when Daddy takes you down to the room to sleep you will wake up better."

"Mommy, will *you* take me down to the room?"

"That's a better idea Annie, Mommy *will* take you down to the room, won't you Mommy? You're better at that than me."

Niamh turns and looks straight at me, frowning slightly and reaches down and pinches me on the inside upper leg as she says, "Okay Annie, Mommy will bring you down to the room." She smiles as I rub the inside of my leg and Annie laughs at my over-reaction to the pinch. And so, we all laugh together and though brief, it feels good.

Mags, the nurse, arrives over to the bedside with another woman following behind.

"Anthony, this is Marie, she's a counsellor and therapist and she's here, as I told Niamh last night, to help you with any needs, or enquiries, throughout this time."

"Hello Marie, how are you?" I say as we shake hands. A fair haired, middle-aged woman with a pleasant look about her.

"Hello Anthony, nice to meet you."

Mags pulls over a chair.

"Sit down Marie, Niamh, I'll bring the consent form shortly for you to read over and sign. Call me if you need anything else."

"Okay Mags, thanks."

Annie lies on her side with her back to us with Snowy cuddled into her neck.

"Now guys if there's anything you want to talk about, any questions you want to ask, any concerns at all, please feel free, that's what I'm here for."
Niamh looks at Marie then scoots her chair closer and whispers "I'm worried about the risks Marie. Of the surgery."

Marie, in a whisper replies "You will always have that with surgery, Niamh. She will be in good hands with Doctor Timmins and his team. This is the only option."

I don't like this, I don't want to listen to this chat, I hoped Niamh wouldn't start asking about risks.

"She's seven now, isn't she? Well, you know she could have had this growing from birth even. There's a possibility she could have been born with the tumour and..." I interrupt Marie at this point.

"You know she was born on New-Year's day Marie? In the early hours of 2005."

"Really? Oh, very good. At what time?" Marie's eye's narrow a little as she searches my face. "5.30 am. It was the quietest New Year I ever saw in. I was actually speeding on the Lucan bypass, heading for Holles Street Hospital as the countdown began on the radio. Niamh was doing counting on her own, between contractions. By the time we got to the quays, in the city, the revellers were out in force. They were spilling out of the bars and clubs, into the street. When I was stopped at a red light, they were knocking on the windows and wishing us a happy New Year, probably thinking we were a miserable pair, with our look of panic and pain. But a Happy New Year it turned out to be for us. As those parties gradually lost tempo, as sheer exhaustion was bringing the celebrations to an end, life was only beginning for Annie and of course, the start of parenthood for Niamh and myself."

"Ahh...that's a lovely story. He's a bit of a storyteller Niamh, is he?"

"Oh, don't get him started Marie, he won't stop."

Mags returns with the consent form. "I need you both to read and sign this, please," she says. With Niamh at my shoulder, I tick all the boxes to the questions and sign the bottom.

"What's the date Niamh?" I say,

"I don't know, with everything that's been going on."

"It's the third of April," Marie says

"It's what!" I ask?

"Third of April," she repeats. "Are you serious, my God, it is too," I say, as Niamh put her hand over her mouth. "Why? Why is that significant?" Marie asks.

SHARDEND BIRMINGHAM

APRIL 3rd 1981

I stood at the gates of Guardian Angels School, laughing at John who was doing an impression of our teacher Mr Riley.

"No running in the corridors you…oh shit, there's my bus Ant, gotta go, see you Monday."

"See you John," I stated as I watched him run for his bus, with the tail of his shirt hanging out below his grey jumper. I kept watching because I knew with John the show was never over. He got on the double-decker bus then ran to the back, downstairs, and squeezed in between two old ladies and squashed his face up to the window with his tongue out. And he stayed that way till the bus disappeared around the bend of Packinton Avenue.

"What are you laughing at Ant?" Jimmy asked, as he approached with Steve.

"I'm laughing at John on the bus, pulling faces between two old ladies."

"He's a laugh, he is."

"Come on lads, let's go home," Steve said, walking and kicking his Umbro bag as he held the shoulder straps out in front of him.

Jimmy, Steve and myself were friends from both school and the estate. We played in the school football team and a Sunday league team. We made dens and climbed trees and all that stuff too, but football was priority. On school days Steve called to my house first and we met Jimmy at Long-Meadow Crescent in the mornings, and he'd split from there to his home in the evenings. Jimmy was tall with brown curly hair and a brilliant goalkeeper. Steve had a shock of flaxen hair and like me, hated wearing his national health glasses, so we kept them in our pockets. Steve had no trouble getting into every football team he trialed for. He had a lethal left foot and understood all the rules of the game. He took it a lot more seriously than the rest of us. Jimmy and I just had to work that bit harder. It was dry but clouds concealed the sunshine as we strolled the tree-lined footpaths of YorksWood council estate, swinging our school bags and kicking any stone in our path on our journey home.

"Thank God it's Saturday tomorrow," Steve said.

"I know yeah, what shall we do?" I asked, as I shouldered Steve over so I could kick the can in front of him.

Steve looked from me to Jimmy "We could have a kick about in the park, we could try and get a few more kids together and organise a game."

"You really, really love football, don't you Steve?" Jimmy said.

27

"Yeah, I'm gonna be a professional when I grow up."

I stopped walking, to draw attention, and the two boys looked back curiously at me. "Well, I'm gonna be an actor, cos when I was six, I wanted to be a cowboy, then at seven I wanted to be in the army, then last year I wanted to be a detective. But now I know if I just go to America and become an actor and get in the films, then I can be all of those things, you know what I mean?"

"Well your Dad tells everyone you're gonna be a priest, Ant," Steve said and we all laughed.

"No way, no way, it's up to me and I'm gonna be in the films."

Jimmy swung his bag over his shoulder as we neared Long Meadow Crescent. "I'm gonna be a racing driver, definitely. See you in the morning lads, I'll call for ya about half ten Ant,"

"Okay."

Steve made a salute with his palm. "See ya Jimmy. I'm starved Ant, I hope it's fish'n'chips for dinner this evening."

"I don't know what ours will be, or who's cooking it, 'cos there's someone different every evening. The best one was our Aunty Bridget from Chicago who flew over last week. She made these homemade American burgers, they were lovely."

"When's your mom gonna get better, Ant?"

"I don't know, soon I think 'cos she went to Lourdes and they washed her in the miracle Holy water and that, so she should start getting better soon." We approached the back alley that led to the rear of our house. "If I'm allowed out Steve, I'll call over to you after dinner, okay mate?"

"Okay Ant, see you later."

I was greeted inside the gate by Pompey, our little Jack Russel terrier, wagging her butty tail.

We lived on the end row of terraced houses, the end houses were the larger four-bedroom ones and with four girls and two boys each room had a comfortable two occupants. The house and its location, with nearby parks and lakes, appealed to Dad, who drove a Hymac excavator on the estate during its construction in the early seventies.

A bespectacled handsome man, Dad emigrated from County Roscommon in 1957 and drove buses around Birmingham before going into construction. He met my mother, a native of county Mayo in 1963 in a Birmingham dancehall for ex-Pats, called 'The Shamrock'. Their romance concluded in matrimony the following year and they resided in a one bedroom flat on Bromley Lane, Erdington. Nine months from their wedding day, Jacqueline was born. The following year Shane was born.

When Mom became pregnant a year later it was time to move to larger accommodation, a maisonette in King's Hurst, Solihull, which was home for the next six years, in which time my sisters Michelle, Tracey and I were born. So with dad having one eye on a house at the end of the row in the new housing estate he was working on, and his children growing nearly as fast as they were getting born, it was time to make the last move to Yorkswood, Shardend. We were in the house four years in the summer of 1977 when the fourth girl and baby of the family Mary Louise was born.

I was well used to a lot of adults coming and going from our house since Mom became ill the previous year. There were so many they moved her down to the living-room into a big hospital bed for convenience. There was always a Holy candle lit upon the mantelpiece, its little glow dancing below the Sacred Heart picture, and this particular evening was no different. There were aunts and uncles from both sides who all resided in various parts of England. It wasn't just relatives. Mom made a lot of her own friends down the years who called in and tried to help as much as they could, as did Mary and Frank next door.

The headmaster of my school, Joe Brennan was visiting most days too, with our Parish Priest, Father Cotter. On occasions Joe would set up a slide show of images for Mom and the rest of us, that Dad brought back from Lourdes of bronze life size sculptures of The Stations of the Cross.

But my excitement of a slide show would be well worn off by the Lord's first fall, by which time I'd have no choice but to sit it out. It always amused me how the gathering would divide on Dad's announcement of a reciting of the rosary. Usually those of Irish origin would edge forward towards the Sacred Heart picture reaching in their pockets for rosary beads while the locals would suddenly mumble their excuses and slip into a reverse step and make for the door. It got better when one or two of the genuinely warm-hearted locals who never practised the Catholic faith got caught up at the front of the room near Mom's bed as the crowd pushed forward and Dad began a vociferous five decades of the rosary. By bedtime, most of the crowd would disperse. This night, however, they were slow to do so. After kissing my sleeping mother, then doing the rounds of trying to avoid kissing everyone else, I went to bed and slept myself.

Early morning, April fourth and it was barely bright when Tracey woke me by removing Andy Grey, my beloved bear that Mom won at bingo, from under my arm.

"Hey, what you doing?"

"Get up, Ant. Let's go downstairs."

"Why?"

"There's people down there, listen." Tracey sat on my bed and cocked her head to listen. I sat up and did the same.

"Oh yeah, what's going on?"

"Sssh, don't wake Shane," Tracey said as we both looked at the big heap in the next bed. I climbed out, wearing my Villa kit for pyjamas.

"I'll race you downstairs to see Mom," Tracey said.

Tracey and I were competitive with each other, with her tomboy ways and her two years

31

senior to me, she remained a test. So, the pushing and shoving started immediately across the landing and down the stairs. But just before we got our hands on the living-room door, Aunt Margaret shouted from the phone table in the hall.

"Don't go in there."

"Why?" Tracey said.

"We want to say good morning to Mom," I said.

"I'll have to call you back," Aunt Margaret said into the phone and placed it down and then, walked towards us. A dark-haired woman of slight build, her stern ways concealed at times her kind heart.

"You can't go in there this morning. Your mother's resting, good girl, good boy. Now upstairs 'till you're told to come down."

We ascended the stairs reluctantly and set about waking Michelle to tell her there was something weird going on downstairs. So, for the next while, we just looked down from the window and watched as visitors assembled at our home earlier than usual.

A new Jaguar pulled up with a private registration J.D.CON.

"It's Jack and Bridie Donnelly," I shouted.

"Yeah, what they doing here?" Michelle said. Just then, Dad came into the bedroom.

"Michelle, Tracey, Anthony. Get dressed. You're going to Jack Donnelly's for breakfast.

"Good morning Dad," I said.

"Oh, good morning, sorry," he said as he came over and held and kissed us all "Now, come on, get ready."

Jack and Bridie Donnelly were my godparents and we always enjoyed when Mom and Dad would pay a visit. Their home was larger than we were used to, with a never-ending supply of crisps, pop, and sweets. With their relaxed hospitality having an immediate influence on Mom and Dad, we never wanted to go home.

After breakfast in Jack and Bridie's home, they took the three of us to nearby Sutton and straight into a bakery where Jack told us to pick any cake in the shop that we wanted.

"One each?" Michelle asked.

"Oh yes, and did you ever have fresh cream? It's delicious," Bridie said. So, with three large fresh cream cakes in large bags, the three of us salivating, we left the shop, as Jack instructed us not to eat them yet.

"We'll put them in the fridge 'till later, sure, we have a few more things to do first. The big race is on today, the Grand National, so we'll go home and we'll all pick a horse and I'll put a pound on each of them but you keep your winnings if your horse comes in."

"Oh, cool," Tracey said.

As peculiar as the morning was, my sisters and I just went along with the sheer thrill of it all. Having left our fresh cream cakes in their fridge and circled a few horses on the newspaper, we set off again in the car. First to the Bookies where Jack placed our bets. Then back to our own home.

"We'll just pop in for a short while," Jack said as he parked the big Jag in the only space left near our house. As happy as we were confused, we leapt out of the car to tell Mom and Dad about our morning. We weaved through the crowds that had spilt out onto the front garden and we met Dad at the door. Only then, I knew something was very wrong. Everyone was sad, people were looking at me and crying. Dad put his arms around us and led us into the living room and up to Mom's bed as he said. "Mommy's died and gone to heaven."

I stood looking at my thirty-eight-year old mother, rosary beads clasped in her joined hands. I climbed the high bed a little and kissed her face, the coldness of her cheeks took me by surprise. It was then that I wept along with my sisters.

As the morning stretched in to a dull-grey afternoon, Michelle, Tracey, and I left again in the car with Jack and Bridie, before the Undertaker arrived. In their home, Jack and Bridie tried desperately to lighten our spirits and our devastated souls but we were unable to even consider the fresh cream cakes placed before us or heed the grand national on the T.V. We returned home that evening. The living-room had a hollow feeling, it seemed bare with the big bed removed, and furniture was rearranged the same as a time before, that seemed long ago, a time that could *never* be the same. Over the next few days, the chaos at home remained, with people coming and going and the six of us hanging around the house. We tried to console each other if one of us started to cry, but it would only start us all off again. Then gradually, over the days, our weeping became sporadic. Mary Louise, at three, played her usual games, pleased to be reunited with her siblings after being with a neighbour's family for two days. She played, oblivious to her loss.

Over these days I thought of bedside conversations I had with my mother over the last few months, how she would keep telling me to be good.

"Be a good boy, be a good boy for Daddy. Try your best to be good. Make sure to keep going to mass and be good."

Now I understood. I thought of my brother and sisters and how I was happy to have them. I felt safe with my family and Dad most of all. It was after two days that I began to feel my strength return.

As a serving altar boy, I wanted to serve Mom's funeral mass. It was on the third day I approached Dad in the kitchen. I watched him as he stood staring out through the net curtained window to the back garden, leaning on the empty countertop, palms down but fingers closed in tight. Lennon's *Imagine* on the radio was being drowned out, as the boiling kettle on the blue flame began its whistle. I knocked off the gas and lifted a small cup from the draining board and slid it in front of him. He looked down at me, smiling up at him.

"Ahh, Anthony do you want a cup of tea? I'm making a pot, one sugar isn't it?" he said, his expression softening.

"Yes, thanks Dad. Dad can I serve Mom's funeral mass?"

"Okay, er, okay son but you'll have to ask Joe Brennan, and he'll talk to Father Cotter. Sure, why don't you walk up to the school now? It's a fine day and all."

"Okay Dad."

I was glad to be out of the house and to have a purpose for the first time in a few days, with the sun shining I had a spring in my stride. I felt pleased, pleased that I wasn't feeling as low as the last few days. A little over halfway, just outside the estate, a tall thin old man was slowly walking towards me with his grocery shopping in plastic and paper carrier bags. As I was getting closer towards him a paper carrier gave way and released its oranges all over the pavement, rolling in different directions. My first thought was to keep my head down and keep on going, till I looked up at the desperate expression on his face. So, I gathered the oranges from the pavement and gutter, we found room in his plastic carrier and he put some into his jacket pockets then he offered me one.

"No, thank you."

"Well thank you very much young man you're a good lad."

"Okay bye," I said.

Feeling awkward, I broke into a little trot for a few yards, then a quick walk. I glanced back but I couldn't see the man, so I searched my pockets and fished out my glasses. I had to hold them to my eyes as one arm was missing, as though one would with binoculars, and I spotted him, entering the old aged pensioners centre and I was happy I helped him.

Guardian Angels school is a single storey sprawl with both infants and juniors in one building. The playgrounds sit to the rear, away from the road, with the church to the right, all enclosed by a perimeter steel rail. Before I knocked the door with Headmaster on it, I waited and thought of what I was going to say. I could hear Mrs. Dodd the secretary typing fast in her office to the left, click, click, click, click, click, click, ding, ziiiiiiiiiip, click, click. The school was relatively peaceful for its occupants, apart from the distant echo of a teachers raised pitch. All lessons were on, and I was pleased to be spared of them.

"Come in," Joe Brennan said as I knocked.

Though I'd got used to him as someone around our house, I knew he would be in Headmaster mode now. "Excuse me Mr. Brennan I ..."

"Ahh Anthony, how are you today?"

He rose from behind his desk and pulled up two seats on the other side.

"Sit down, sit down Anthony, what can I do for you?"

"Sir… sir I was wondering if I could serve the alter at my Mom's funeral mass?"

A slender man with grey hair and black rimmed glasses. He looked at me and said,

"Will you be okay with it, Anthony?"

"Yes sir."

"Then I'll see to it."

"Thank you, sir."

"Good lad."

They gave me the easy duties. I was on bells throughout the mass and holding a candle behind the coffin on its way out. I'd served plenty of funeral masses before this and as I looked down at the crowds who had gathered, there was no doubt this was the biggest. There were two large doors at the back of the church wide open with people trying to get in, and there was easily as many people standing down the wing aisles as there was seated. *I mustn't get upset. I have my duties, they're important.* I remained focused to the end, with my bell ringing on cue and avoiding eye contact with my family. I didn't shed a tear.

When Father Cotter finished mass, just before he stepped down to release the smoking incense, he leaned into the microphone and said,

"I must say, I haven't seen such a crowd since the Pope's visit."

I was one of four boys holding candles behind the coffin as we shuffled down the centre aisle. My focus was strained, but I remained so, through parting crowds outside in the bright morning sunshine, until we reached the shining black hearse, where I blew out my candle.

The next day when Dad told me I was going to Mayo with my sisters Tracey and Mary Louise for a few months, I was only slightly surprised, but very excited. Though I wasn't expecting it at all I was becoming conditioned to take whatever comes along.

"And what about school Dad?"

"You will be back again in time for school in September, with the help of God."

With that, he picked me up and held me and I hugged his neck.

"Oh God bless us and save us. I love you Anthony. Promise you'll be a good boy for Aunt Rose. I have to put you down son you're getting too big for lifting."

Dad placed me down and I stood on my tip toes hugging his belly, as I whispered,

"I will. I love you too Dad."

My mother's sister Rose remained in her home place looking after Granny and cultivating the farm. She played host to all her returning siblings and their growing families at holiday times. With her husband Jimmy and four children they made such a welcome and fuss of us for two weeks every summer, that we found it heart breaking to leave. With Granny not fit to travel, Rose made the trip to Mom's funeral alone, but with three more mouths to feed on her return. We flew from Birmingham to Dublin, where we were picked up and driven for six hours to Rossport village in a mini bus, by Rossports local taxi man / postman amongst other duties Mikey Corduff.

Rossport is a small fishing village in the north-west corner of County Mayo. It is surrounded on three sides by the sea, as its location is at the centre of two main channels that join in to one at the mouth of Broad Haven Bay, which feeds the Atlantic Ocean. When I stepped down from the van onto the meagre road, I got the strong familiar smell of burning turf, a smell that belongs to rural Ireland, to my holidays. I couldn't help but stare as though I had never seen the view before. I slipped my glasses from my pocket and held them to my eyes and looked down at the sloping, lush green pasture in front of me. It held a thicket of gorse in its centre, like trespassers, as they swayed their yellow bloom in the breeze with entitlement. The bay waters rippled out below the land, skimming the curvature of the coast and the rocky shores on the other side, beneath the expansive mountain that upheaved the skyline. A narrow road skirted the mountain, linking a graveyard, a pub, and several homesteads whose chimneys plumed and curled silver smoke in agreement.

"You wouldn't get that view in Birmingham."

I turned to see the weathered handsome face of Jimmy, a tall wiry man, and a brother of Mikey.

"Hello Uncle Jimmy," I said as I slipped my glasses away and gave him a hug

"I'm sorry for your troubles young man, I really am, I'm sorry."

I looked up at Jimmy and saw his bright blue eyes filling. He took my hand and led me to the house.

"Come on, there's people inside that want to meet ye."

It felt good to be around Aunt Rose and Granny at this time and we had a maternal attachment to both. Mary Louise bonded in no time with her cousin Rosaleen who was also three. The hospitality we received not only from our own family but the people of Rossport was momentous. Tracey and I attended the local school for the last term where we were taught Irish, thirty-three years after our mother began attending the old school across the road as an Irish speaker to learn English. Every home was a farm with cows, sheep, donkeys, chickens, geese, ducks, and dogs. With the new environment and making more friends it all acted as a positive distraction. When the school term finished, Tracey was capable of reading and writing a few sentences in Irish, but I, only through the desperation of a straining bladder was able to ask permission to use the toilet.

The summer holidays brought long bright days of fun, but I had my duties also, which I carried out daily. I collected the cows from the fields in the morning for milking in the sheds, then after, I would let them up the mountain behind the house for the day, then gather them again that evening and put them back in the field for the night. After some practise I learned to milk one of the smaller cows, after more practise again I managed to prevent her from kicking over my bucket of hard-earned milk. I remember my first success, dreamily strolling back down the boreen to show off my half-full bucket to Aunt Rose and Granny in the house, after an hour of sitting on a stool amongst the piss, shit and flies, pulling and squeezing on the teats of a bulging udder. A donkey in the field leaned over the fence as I passed and looked to the heavens and released a savage, harsh, ear-piercing bray. It lifted me with fright, and I brought my arms up in a moment of terror and let go of the bucket around chest height and with the donkey still in full cry I dropped to my knees and caught it with both arms in a chest hug before it landed and only lost the splash over my face. Mikey in the post van brought me letters from friends at home with newspaper cuttings about Aston Villa becoming League Champions and my excitement would turn to homesickness for a short while, but there was too much going on to be lonely, the days passed quickly.

It was Wednesday 29 July, and Aunt Rose and Granny were watching the royal wedding of Prince Charles and Lady Diana Spencer on the television. I was invited to a birthday party at the end of the road.

"Are you coming Ant?" Tracey said.

"Who's is it?"

"It's a girl called Niamh, she's five and there's gonna be pop and crisps and ice-cream and jelly and cakes."

"And who else is going?"

"Mary Louise, Rosaleen, Maura, Marion, Nora and Theresa."

"No thanks, too many girls for my liking."

I do regret not going to the party. But not because of the of the treats Tracey tried to tempt me with. But because there was a group photo taken that day of all those that attended and it would have been notable to have been in a photo at that time, with my future wife.

Mid-August and Dad arrived in Rossport with Jackie, Shane, and Michelle in a car he borrowed from his friend Dennis Keenahan. The reunion felt good. I missed Michelle a lot but the five and six years between Shane, Jackie and I, remained a cordial distance. It seemed, in the few months since I last saw them, they had both grown fast. Shane was taller and had a step cut into the back and sides of his hair and a long fringe that covered one of his eyes. He also adopted a different walk with a noticeable swagger as his feet splayed out at ten to two on the dial.

"Shane's a Mod now Ant," Michelle said.

"What's a Mod?"

"Someone who acts modern and listens to

music by the Specials and Madness and that."

"Oh"

"And have a guess what," she whispered in my ear.

"He smokes and drinks cider too. But don't tell Dad."

"Is Jackie a mod as well?"

"No, but her boyfriend Mark is."

A week later, we left Rossport with aching hearts. Mary Louise, Tracey, and I sobbed for the first part of the journey through Mayo before eventually settling. I lay back in my window seat and tried to familiarize cloud shapes for a while, but the six of us being together again wouldn't allow such withdrawal. Shane started singing 'Ghost town' from the front passenger seat and Jackie, seated behind him, mumbled along in approval.

"Do you like 'This ole house' Ant, Shakin Stephens?" Michelle said, nudging me.

"It's gotta be Two Tone man, it's gotta be Two Tone." Shane said craning.

"I like The Specials." I said, looking for Shane's approval

By the time we got to Kilmore, Roscommon, to Dad's homeplace for a two-day visit, I was feeling happy to be with my family again, but a little sardined. The landscape was flatter and more open than Rossport, with trees along the roads and around the farms. Dad drove slowly up a narrow road that had a strip of grass growing all along the middle, till we got to a tall bungalow on its own with small trees and shrubs around its periphery, it was just off the road with enough space to park the length of the short car. In the open doorway stood Nanny Mary with an apron tied around her waist and a great smile that narrowed her eyes, a tall thin woman with grey hair tied to the back of her head in a bun and encased with a net.

As with my granny in Mayo, she was widowed, and Dad's brother Hughie was the one out of ten siblings that remained at home. Hughie came out from the house behind her, a small hardy looking man with a happy crooked grin. There were hugs and tears and kisses and more hugs where we were bumping into one another, I hugged Dad at one point then, embarrassed, backed off. I noticed five buckets of water in a line at the door. *In case of a fire?* Straight inside the door was the kitchen with a shiny concrete floor, an extendable table at the wall on the right and a large open fireplace opposite, where fresh turf was smoking and sparkling as it smothered over a bed of flickering glowing ember.

There was a chair at both fire sides, one soft, and dented to Nanny Mary's shape. At the far end of the kitchen was an open wooden staircase. Under the stairs was a stove and another bucket of water on a stool, beside a basin on a low table. That's when I remembered, unlike my previous digs, this house still relied on the well for its water supply and the toilet was a tin stall down the back garden or a squat around the periphery. At the top of the stairs were two bedrooms built in to the attic, Nanny Mary's was a small one on the left of the short landing, the other was ours, all of us, except Hughie, who's bedroom was down off the kitchen. Our room had two double beds both tucked under either side of the sloping roof and a window in the middle on the gable wall. The bed selection was simply gender based. As the girls unpacked, Dad and Shane sat in the kitchen talking with Nanny Mary and Hughie.

I took a walk around the house, following a path of worn ground. At the back it led away from the house down past a clothesline, and it got narrower as brambles and nettles lined its route. *I miss everyone in Rossport. What are they doing now? Probably sitting down for dinner. But I miss my friends at home too, I even miss school. I just want to go home now, even though Mommy's gone. It's going to be strange.* I stopped at the three-sided toilet, with corrugated metal roof, inside was a short bench with a rough circular hole cut out of it and a bucket beneath it. *Well, there's no mystery to this toilet system.* To one side of the bench lay a neat stack of scissor cut newspaper squares. I took a piss outside of it, into the growth.
I'll only use that for shits, so I don't have to look in to it. When I returned to the kitchen everyone was seated around the extended table eating a feed of chicken, potatoes, and veg. In the hearth, flames now engulfed the turf in a dance, reaching and tapering.

"There's Anthony now," Hughie said rising to his feet with an empty plate. "Sit in here gossoon, I've eaten enough."

"Thankyou." He ruffled my hair as he let me in to his seat.

"That's a fine head of hair. I had a gruaig like that once too when I was a gossoon, didn't I Mammy?

I looked up at Hughie's thin wispy hair, with its low parting, then to Nanny Mary who was just looking at Dad as she slowly ate.

"Well Josie, myself and yourself are going for a walk very shortly," Hughie said heading down to his room.

"Aagh well, if you insist," Dad said smiling. "Will you be okay Mammy?" Dad rubbed the back of Nanny Mary's hand and she placed her other on his.

"Sure, of course I will Josie, the girleens can help me clean up."

"Where are you going, Dad?" Tracey asked shyly.

"The pub." Shane answered. "Can I come with you, Dad?"

"No." Dad said firmly.

Nanny Mary told us stories, Irish folklore, and some of her own, as we all sat on the chairs, brought closer to the fireplace. Mary Louise was sleeping up in the girl's bed in at the wall where the sloped ceiling started. We ate Tayto crisps and drank red lemonade, as the stories got a little scary. When she asked if we had heard of the Banshee I got up and said I was tired, Tracey followed me. I made a ball of myself in the big cold bed and faced into the wall to give Tracey privacy getting changed.

"Oh no."

"What's up?" I said without moving.

"I need a wee."

I turned around quickly leaning on my elbow, she was sitting up on the far bed, beside the lamp that lit the room, "I think I do too, what we gonna do?"

"There's a potty under this bed, Michelle found it earlier, that's what you have to do here. Turn back round, Ant, I gotta go."

"Okay, I'm gonna cover my ears with pillows."

I stayed with my head under the pillow and my hands closing each end into my ears till Tracey tapped me on the shoulder.

"You can go now Ant."

"Thanks."

I got down with a knee either side of the pink potty and squinted. It was half full.

"Did you do all that wee, Trace?

"No way! Michelle did one earlier."

I pissed and the sound of my piss stream hitting the contents of the potty and splashing, filled the room, along with Tracey giggling. I made sure I strained. *I don't want to go later when everyone is in the room.* I went back to bed and curled in a ball facing the wall, but I couldn't sleep, then I heard Michelle, Jackie and Shane running up the stairs, the girls were shrieking as Shane was howling like a banshee. But they quietened when they saw us sleeping or pretending. Shane got in behind me, and the way he fixed the blanket on himself, it totally covered my head, his breathing was fast and heavy in the silence of the room. Then he farted, giggles came from the girl's bed and a smell from ours. But I stayed still. He started whispering.

"Hey Jackie, I'm going out for one, in that toilet out the back."

"Save me two's and I'll go when you come back but hurry up 'cos I think I want a wee as well."
I stayed curled up as he went down the stairs and I gently pulled the blanket off my face. I heard the deep drone of his voice say something to Nanny Mary, then the old door clatter. *I wonder if Tracey is awake. Why am I still awake? Why am I so fascinated by Shane and Jackie?* After a few minutes Jackie broke the silence of the room whispering. "Hurry up, Shane." She walked the creaking boards to the window, closer to me. Then I heard the trickle of her pissing in the potty, the soft splashing filled the room. *I wish I was asleep.* I felt an itch on my head, but I couldn't scratch it, I imagined a spider climbing through my hair. The soft splashing kept going. *If she doesn't stop soon it's going to be…*

"Eeew, oh no." Jackie shrieked. Then a loud grinding from the window.
"What's that, what you doin' Jack?" Tracey asked.
So, I turned around and grabbed my glasses, pretending to be woken. I saw the potty on the floor full to the brim and a puddle around it and Jackie in her nightie, sliding the bottom half of the

49

window upwards, the room filled with the cold night.

"Nothing, I just need some fresh air. Go back to sleep."

Tracey sat up in the bed, Michelle lifted her head then down again and turned in to Marylouise against the wall. Jackie bent down and gently lifted the potty with one hand on its handle and pinching the lip on the other side as she took tiny steps. It reminded me of the end of term egg and spoon races we had at school. "Fuck it," she whispered as it swayed and spilt out on her hand while she stretched across the wide sill.

She seemed to be in slow motion. With the orange light of the lamp on her back and the dark blue night on her front. She reached out but didn't pour it, she flung it wide, still holding the handle, as the toss of piss scattered straight out, releasing steam, then plummeting in the darkness.

"Aaaagh, for fuck sake, what 'yer doing?" Came Shane's roar from below the window.

"Sorry, I thought you were at the toilet." Jackie said leaning out.

"It's too fucking dark down there. I'm soaked. What was that?"

"It was… just water."

"Is that a potty in your hand, urgh no, for fuck sake yer dirty bitch."

I fell back laughing as Jackie pulled the window down hard and jumped in to bed between Tracey and Michelle, who were laughing too, I lay on my back with the soles of my feet pressed against the sloped ceiling, my hands on my stomach and I couldn't stop. My face, a mess of tears and snot, but it felt so good.

After two days we continued on to Birmingham in time for school again. But not before breaking down in Hollyhead as we exited the ferry. We sat squashed together on the roadside with steam escaping from under the bonnet.

"Well fuck it anyways," Dad said, as he searched for ten pence pieces for phone calls.

"Shane, did you take those ten pence pieces from here?" Dad said, as he pointed down at the empty tray besides the gear-stick, and looked at Shane beside him.

"No, I didn't," Shane said, as he turned and viewed the Welsh countryside.

It seemed an eternity before Frankie Beckett from next door arrived in his van with a tow rope and pulled us home to Yorkswood. The hysteria had started.

Back home and unpacking in my room I came across my bear Andy Grey, which I'd left behind in a hurry. His furry chest was torn wide open and his stuffing of diced sponge was spilling out of him. I carried him down to Dad in the kitchen. "Dad, what happened to Andy?" I held him out so he could see the damage, as he stood stirring a cup of tea. "Oh, that was Pompey, she was on-heat there for a while and I couldn't let her out, every dog in the estate was around the back gate. I caught her up on Andy a few times." I looked at Shane sitting at the table with tea and toast.

"I don't know what you mean, Dad."

"I told you that you were too old for a teddy ages ago," Shane said.

Dad saw I was upset. "What's on-heat mean?" Dad looked at Shane, then back to me and stooped down in front of me and rubbed my shoulder "Sorry Anthony, Pompey was fighting with it. But you're a big boy now anyway."

"Yeah okay."

"Good lad." He rubbed my head. "Give him to me now and I'll put him away." I passed Andy over and went back upstairs.

Granny and Aunt Rose are in the kitchen and the house is busy with people. Shane and my sisters play with kids around the farm. Mommy takes my hand. "C'mon, my little maneen, you can come visiting with me." I hold her hand as we walk the Rossport road. No footpath's or kerbs. And I jump the cowpats that are all along the road. We visit homes of nice people who smile at me. I turn my face into Mommy's skirt.

This is Anthony Michael she tells them all. An old man with a smelly smoky pipe gives me pop and crisps and his wife says, "you're from your mother's side". *She must mean her belly.* After the visits we walk back along the road, but not holding hands, because I'm running, then flying, flying up over and across the fields and haycocks then down along the shore, gliding like a bird across the strand. But not over the mountain, I'm too tired to go on. So, Mommy carries me, and I sleep at her neck. I wake as she puts me on a bed and takes off my trainers. Then my eyes close again as she kisses my cheek.

2012
IN THE NAME OF LOVE

Early morning April fourth, I lie in bed thinking about Annie in intensive care after her surgery. Relieved to see the last of the night, as brightness eventually starts to filter through the blinds. But it's still too early for those sleeping. So, I get dressed quietly, trying not to tread the creaking spots. The morning is fine and dry as I close the back door behind me and walk to the forest at the rear of my home, the open grounds of Castletown House. In contemplation, I follow the preferred trodden trail which leads me to an opening where the forest ends, and the grassland starts.

With the great Palladian mansion in sight, I walk through knee high grass, my jeans absorbing droplets of dew, and turn suddenly to the sound of a thousand whispers as I sight a large gathering of starlings performing a murmuration above the tops of the sycamore trees. Like black mist, growing and alive, it casts a shadow on the meadow around me, as they perform shapes, long, wide, but always grouped, never apart. Immediately I think of Annie waking and looking for us. *Our baby needs us.* And so, I head back for home.

It seems everyone in the house slept lightly. Dad and Tracey, Niamh's parents, John and Mary, her sister Rachel and husband Steve, all rouse from beds, couches and armchairs, as I enter, and the grind of the kettle jug quietens to a low rumbling and clicks off. Mikey and Luke spring to life and charge down the stairs.

The morning sun is shining from the south side of Temple street illuminating the elegant spire of St George's church on the north. Niamh and I sit in chairs hunched over, our arms resting on Annie's empty hospital bed. Our backs to the windows. We wait apprehensively. Then Niamh finally speaks.

"Are you prepared for this, Ant?"

"What do you mean?"

"I mean, do you realise she may never be the same child she was, either physically or psychologically, or both. I'm just saying we *have* to be prepared for anything here."

"I'm prepared for anything Niamh, as long as she lives, but I'm not prepared to lose her. I have to grasp on to hope."

Niamh places her hand over the back of mine and rubs it. I feel childlike for a moment. The sound of the ward door opening, its draft excluders sweeping against the lino, snaps us to attention, and we rise to our feet as Annie is pushed through in a wheelchair, by a smiling Mags with Lailani in tow, wheeling a drip feed to Annie's arm. Annie squints at the sunshine on her pale freckled face, her head heavily wrapped with a white bandage and her long auburn hair, moist and draping down below to her shoulders. Her entrance catches the attention of the father and two mothers of the three children sharing the ward. They smile with us as Annie is pushed closer to the end of her bed. Niamh and I rush to her and kneel either side, kissing her face, her arms, her hands, as she attempts a smile, the corners of her mouth curling slightly but her eyes remaining serious and ill looking. The nurses place Annie on the bed, in tandem. Mags fixes her night dress as Lailani makes alterations to the drip and sets up a pulse monitor.

The morning passes quickly, and we remain much the same, seated at Annie's bedside but with not much talk between us. I catch Niamh's eye at times, and she squeezes my hand with a half-smile and we watch Annie as she sleeps. My thoughts are meditative. *It's times like this we realise how fragile we really are. How much of daily living rests upon chance. When things are going well it seems that a multitude of small things, are all falling in to place perfectly to create what we may call a normal day. But time proves these to be the better days. The better days, but we don't feel the happiness that we should on these days, it seems to take an outside view inward, a snapshot or a friend's opinion or others and our own suffering, to realise happiness can carry an expiry date called complacency.*

Early afternoon and we are approached by a tall fair-haired lady, a social worker called Una McCluskey. She wants to chat to us later in the evening, so a meeting is arranged for 5pm that evening. And with her help Niamh arranges visits of our families to briefly see Annie.

"What's that all about Niamh? What does she want to talk about?" I say as Una leaves the ward.

"Well, I'd say she's going to address all the changes we may or may not have to adapt to. Depending on the outcome."

"What changes?"

"You know Ant, this is what I was talking about earlier. I don't think you're prepared for what could be in store here."

I meet Dad, Tracey, John, Mary, and Rachel in reception in the evening.

"Steve's waiting in the car Ant, he can't f nd a parking spot so he's going to keep moving around," Rachel says.

"Sure, we won't be that long at all, just in and out," Mary says as she links John's arm.

"You go ahead Anthony and lead the way, good man," John says.

We stand at the reception outside the ward door as I explain to them how the bedside visits have to be two people, then two, then the one, and to be as brief as possible, and that Niamh and myself are going to meet the social worker. I lead John and Mary to Annie's bed side as Niamh gives up her chair. Annie looks up and smiles. A smile that breaks a set face, eye lids heavy, lips dry, but a smile, as she speaks in a whisper.

"It's Nanny and Gaga."

Annie's earliest attempts at Grandad has affectionately being carried on.

Down the corridor of the ward Una leads us into a

small empty staff canteen, where we sit at a table.

"Niamh, Anthony how are you coping?"

I look at Niamh and I can see the question makes her emotional.

Her quivering chin is always the start. So, I answer.

"We're as good as can be expected. You know we're over the first hurdle so to speak."

"That's right," Una says as she hands Niamh tissues from a box on the table.

"I'm fine, I'm fine," she says taking the tissues. "I just didn't want Annie seeing me upset like this. I suppose I've being bottling things up a little, and I'm a bit tired to be honest."

"It's good to have a cry Niamh. Don't bottle it up. Are you staying in the hospital over night or going home?"

"I'm sleeping in the ward beside Annie. But I'm fine, really."

"Maybe you could take it in turns. Anthony, you could give her a rest."

"I have no problem with that..."

"No, I wouldn't have it any other way. Besides, I'd definitely not sleep at home away from Annie. Really I'm fine."

"Okay, I know you're both aware the next hurdle is the big one, the test results of the tumour, and you have to be as prepared as you can for the worse result. If its malignant, then it's going to bring a lot of changes to your familiar routine in life. You'll have to forget for the short term about work, the mortgage, and the bills. We can send correspondence to put these things on hold for a while, till you adjust over the coming weeks. Use your family and friends for as much support as you can. If the result is malignant, we will work together as a team to do whatever we have to, to make things easier. But there is also as much chance it will be benign." I loosen some tissues from the box and leave the table.

With Niamh at Annie's bedside again, we gather on the pavement beside the steps of the hospital entrance. Dad, Tracey, John, Mary, and Rachel all glazy eyed, as Steve pulls in beside us. The tissues are out and there's a feeling of agitation. Dad looks up to the bright evening sky, it gleams on his glasses.

"Well, isn't it mighty weather for this time of year? It's unnatural. I don't remember an April as good."

"Dad, that's about the fiftieth time you've said that in the last week," Tracey says to restrained laughs. I look at her. *Middle aged now. Where did the years go? I can see both our parents in her features.*

"Well, what did you all think of Annie?" I say,

"She's mighty the cretchur, for what she's been through," Mary says.

John nods his head. "Oh, mighty indeed."

"Oh my God, yes," Tracey looks at Mary, "Five and a half hours of brain surgery and she's sitting up in bed trying to smile for everyone. She's my hero."

Rachel hugs me. "Yeah, she's amazing Ant, she

59

really is. Come on guys, we have to get moving, Steve's on double yellow lines."

"Well, I haven't had a drop, the whole Lent. But if I don't get myself in to that car and away from that pub on the corner that's winking at me." Dad points to the Temple Pub. "I'm afraid I'll drink it dry with the thirst I've built up."

Tracey holds Dad's arm and turns him towards the car. "Well, you've only got till Sunday, Dad. So, get in the car you ole git."

We laugh as he stoops and steps into the car.

Back at Annie's bedside I sit with Niamh drinking coffee when Marie the therapist comes over and pulls up a chair.

"Annie's looking great, isn't she? When did she get out of intensive care?"

"About ten this morning," Niamh says.

"And how are you two doing?"

"Not bad. We had my parents and Anthony's Father, and other family members visit today."

"Very good. Did they manage to see Annie?"

"Yeah, just for a short while," Niamh says.

"Oh, that's good, and how is your Father, Anthony?"

"He's good. He's looking forward to Sunday as he's off the beer for lent."

"Ahh, good man himself. I'd say he's strong, mentally I mean, for all he went through."

"Yes, he is, I suppose."

"Did he bring you all up on his own?"

"Oh yeah, he did of course. It was chaotic at times, but he got the job done."

NOVEMBER 1981 SHARDEND

Winter darkness swiftly cloaked the light of the evening, leaving a fusion of yellow and red diminishing beyond the terraced rooftops of Yorkswood housing estate. I walked with my brother and sisters behind Dad as he held Mary Louise's hand, our path lit by street posts.

"Why do we have to go to this place Dad?" Jackie said.

"Because it's the Social Welfare Jacqueline, and they have the power to stop my money. Now hurry on," Dad said.

We came out of the estate and entered the gates of Shardend Park. Michelle, Tracey, and I broke off from the rest to play on the swings.

"Come on, come on, we haven't got time," Dad shouted as he picked Mary Louise up and went in the opposite direction.

Dad was in no mood for messing tonight so we swiftly regrouped. We walked the footpath that followed the curves of Shardend lake, it's waters black and silent, until we emerged at the exit from the park. Which was a short cut to the new estate where the Social Welfare offices were.

A red brick building of three storeys with stone steps leading to the first floor where a glow of white neon read MAIN ENTRANCE. We stood behind Dad in hushed silence on the bright landing at the top of the stairs, Dad searched the door, moving his head around.

"Where the fuck is the knocker on this yolk?"
Shane stepped forward and pressed a buzzer at the side of the door.

"Dad you swore," Tracey said.

"Sorry, sorry," Dad said, just as the door opened. A tall man with a friendly smile and brown wavy hair stood to one side of the doorway, his right arm stretched out.

"Ahh, Joseph Giblin and family, welcome. I'm Richard, Joseph, pleased to meet you."

As he shook Dad's hand a smiling fair-haired woman with glasses appeared behind Richard.

"This is June my colleague, June this is Joseph." Dad stepped into the door way and shook June's hand.

"Joe is fine, Joe will do. And sorry again for leaving it late," he said.

"That's okay. Come on in Joe and introduce us to your family," June said.

We followed Richard and June in to a large bright sitting room of white walls that was sparsely furnished, apart from three couches in the middle, placed in a U shape with a coffee table in the centre of them and two hard chairs at the wall to the left beside a closed door in the corner.

"Sit down and make yourselves comfortable," Richard said.

We all sat around on the couches, Richard

passed a chair to June and pulled one over for himself closing the U shape. I sat close to Tracey and whispered.

"What's a colleague Trace?"

"I don't know, I think it means they're going to get married, Ant."

"Now Joe," June said, as her eyes searched us. "What's everybody's names and ages here?"

"Well, this little one beside me is the baby Mary Louise, she's four, then there's Anthony over there he's nine and Tracey beside him, she's ten …"

"No eleven, Dad, I'm eleven now."

"Sorry Tracey, then there's Michelle she's twelve, Shane there is fourteen and the eldest is Jacqueline beside him at fifteen."

"Oh, very good, you really have your hands full there," June said.

"And you're from Ireland originally, Joe?" Richard asked.

"That's right, I'm from County Roscommon."

"Well, you have a lovely family, every one of them similar with their freckles and blue eyes. Do you mind Joe if we just have a quiet word with you in the next room?" June said.

"No, no problem at all."

Richard and June stood and led Dad through the door in the corner of the room. With the door closed shut, Shane and Jackie got up and stood at the wall with the side of their heads pressed against it. Mary Louise climbed on to the coffee table and jumped onto the couch, then climbed on to the coffee table and jumped on to the couch again, laughing each time she landed, Michelle sat upside down with her legs folded over the back-rest, her long wavy auburn hair draped to the floor, Tracey looked at me and laughed, then grabbed me in a head lock that I managed to squeeze out of, I caught her the same way but she was saved by Shane as he ordered us all to sit quiet.

"Sshh, I'm trying to listen to what they're saying to Dad, just stay quiet."

So, we all sat together in silence watching Shane and Jackie facing each other with their mouths open as they pressed their ears to the wall.

"They're asking how Mom died," Shane whispered.

"Now they want to know if we're all well behaved and…there asking Dad if he's struggling."

We watched as Shane and Jackie concentrated to hear every word and they started to smile at each other, Jackie placed a hand to her mouth to conceal a laugh.

"What's funny, Jackie?" Michelle said.

"Dad's telling them how he was one of eleven kids in a small house that didn't even have running water and the toilet was a makeshift out-building down the garden," Shane whispered.

"And that *we* wouldn't know hunger," Jackie said. Shane and Jackie's expressions changed and a knot formed on Shane's brow.

"What's foster care, Shane, is it a home?" Jackie asked.

"Sshh," Shane said, placing his finger to his lips as he glanced over at us.

Michelle, Tracey and I, caught each other's stare and looked away, shifting in our seats. Mary Louise lay her head down on Michelle's lap. The room went silent for a moment. The door in the corner opened halfway into the other room, and we could see Dad standing with his back to us, giving Shane and Jackie time to settle back down to the couch. We heard him speaking.

"I've heard enough of this, I'll manage, I'll manage just fine if you leave my widower's allowance at me."

Then Dad opened the door fully and walked into the room and sat down beside Michelle, he lifted Mary Louise up and sat her on his lap and held her sleeping head into his chest. We all sat in silence for a few minutes with just the sound of Dad's breathing, which was heavier than usual. June entered the room with a grey rectangular tape recorder in her hands.

"Now Joe and kids, I'm just going to record you. I want you all to have a discussion and to talk openly amongst yourselves about your current situation, about how you feel right now, about your lives at present."

She placed the tape recorder in the middle of the coffee table, then pressed down on the play and record buttons at the same time.

"Okay, I shall be in the other room with Richard and I'll call back in a little while."

As June closed the door in the corner of the room we sat there in silence, not even Dad's breathing could be heard only the faint whirring of the tape recorder going around slowly.

"What did she say Trace, about a present?" I whispered, as Tracey sniggered into her hand.

"Ouch, Shane! Dad tell him he just pinched me, like that." Jackie said, as she demonstrated a revenge pinch on Shane's arm.

"Ow! Jackie, fuck off," Shane said, sniggering as he leant away from her.

"Shane! Watch your language. And behave yourselves, the two of yers," Dad said, with a glance at the tape recorder.

Michelle snorted a laugh through her hand then the room fell silent again for another few minutes. I looked down at the tape with its reels slowly rotating, and I knew that none of us was going to start talking about how we felt, we wouldn't know how to. I blew a big raspberry as hard as I could and said, "Er...excuse me."

Everybody laughed except Dad, who stood up with Mary Louise in his arms and said, "I've had enough of this, come on, put your coats on and we'll go home and say the rosary."

Dad opened the door we had come in, then the door on the landing, and we walked down the stone steps as the reels of the tape rotated. It was a clear November night, with stars dazzling and distant, the moon proud and almost complete as we walked the path around the lake. Mary Louise was awake again now and holding Dads hand.

"Dad, Dad we didn't say goodbye to June and Richard," Tracey said.

"No, we didn't Tracey, but we'll pray for them in our rosary, we'll pray they understand loyalty." In the years that followed my Mother's death we would kneel every evening in the living room facing the sacred heart picture and say the rosary. We were raised with the best intensions, with Heaven in sight, but at times we were capable of raising hell, with occasional rows and battles. The rosary, it seemed, was Dad's way of trying to reinstall a certain amount of normality and most of all, togetherness, at the end of another day that we got through. A lot of the time Shane did his own thing and Dad found him difficult to control, for most of the manners he had before our Mother's death, he abandoned thereafter. My sisters though were all triers, curiously trying to make their own way, but with innocence at stake.

Each one of us endured our heartache, far from all others knowing, in silent misery. We were all a little lost, but lost together, and each personality was a big one, there were no quiet ones, so it was rarely a peaceful house. We were blessed I suppose, in that we were all avid readers, and this *had* to compensate. There were always books being swopped around the house, albeit, some shite ones.

We never went hungry, not like the way Dad told us he did when he was young. Food was scarce at times, but Dad had a knack of making something out of what seemed like nothing. There was the *gibberly gobberly wonder sandwich* when there was bread and what seemed like not much else. He would take out the chopping board and start chopping a large Spanish onion, very finely, then a few tomatoes chopped finely. (Sometimes his own, that adorned every windowsill in an attempt to redden.)

Cheese, chopped finely and mixed together with generous helpings of salad cream, spread evenly on a slice of buttered bread and capped by another slice, cut into quarters and repeated seven or eight times till we began to retreat from the table, wiping a sleeve across our mouths and rubbing our belly's in contentment. Then there was boxty, everyone's favourite, a dish popular in the west of Ireland, and so simple, all we needed was potatoes, flour, and salt.

But it took a particular utensil to perfect boxty, one which I became quite deft in assembling and proudly gifted to all on request. The potatoes (the biggest in the bag, and always spared for boxty) had to be grated into a puree form and the average cheese grater could not achieve this, so I would wait until a large (family size) tin of peas was used and I would open the bottom of the tin in the same way the top was opened, then left with a tube of tin I would neatly cut it down the seam and straighten it out till it became a flat rectangle, I would then place this over a flat piece of timber and with a hammer and nail I would pierce the tin, whereby the hole would push the tin out in four small places on the reverse side, then repeat this process close to the last one in neat rows till all the tin is completely pierced in an orderly fashion, then I'd arch the tin in its length (the rough side out) and I'd have a boxty grater. Over a bowl Dad would grate his peeled potatoes to puree which would naturally redden as the air got to it. Grated, flour was then added with a generous shake of salt and mixed into a paste, then, like pancakes, it was poured on to a heated well-oiled pan and cooked and turned the same way too.

Dad would cut the cake of boxty into segments on a plate and place it in to the middle of the table around which all six of us would be patiently seated and twelve arms would instantly clear the plate of its contents as Dad went about pouring the next one on to the pan. Despite its simplicity of ingredients its delicious taste took the palate by surprise. Dad found it difficult to spare himself for fulltime employment that was offered to him at times by his contractor friends, parenting and the demands of the house made it difficult. He did however do the occasional few days from time to time and one day was a Friday in June, over two years after our Mother's death.

Jimmy, Steve, and I strolled home through the estate, from Guardian Angels school on that warm evening with our jumpers tied around our waists.

"I'm excited about leaving and starting senior school," Jimmy said.

"Yeah, me too it's going to be a bit weird at first cos it's in the opposite direction. I mean, Jimmy, you'll call for Anthony and you'll both call for me and I'll be the first one home in the evening instead of the last."

"Well, my two sisters go to the big school as well, so we can all walk together," I said.

"What about your brother Shane, he goes as well doesn't he?" Jimmy asked.
"Yeah, but he leaves next month, he's got his exams on at the moment."

"So does our Tina," Steve said.

"Okay lads, I'll see you in the morning, I'll call around about ten Ant."

"Okay Jimmy," I said, as we watched him trail of towards his house.

"Bring your caser and we'll have a kick about on long meadow," Steve shouted after him.

"I wonder if our chickens have laid any more eggs for me?" I said,

"Ha, ha, my Mom said its crazy having chickens in a council house."

"I know but you know what our Dad's like, he just went out to a farm in Coleshill to buy fresh eggs and a big bag of spuds and came back with four chickens instead, it's just a laugh, I think it reminds him of his home in Ireland."

"My Mom said the foxes might get them."

"No way, I've built a good pen for them and

they're fenced off and I lock them up every night."

"I love your house, it's a laugh, mine's just boring."

"I'll see you tomorrow Steve," I said, as I reached the back alley of my house.

"See you mate."

I opened the back gate to Pompey's greeting; I knew my entrance had disturbed her thoughts of what she would do if she could get into the fenced area and let loose on those four chickens. Pompey had all the traits of the terrier – one day a friend of Dad's brought two budgies in a cage around to the house and told Dad he could have them as they were *too bloody noisy.*

Dad set them on a table in the corner of the living room and he named them Paddy and Polly. On Sunday evenings after his visit to the Social club for his few pints Dad would take out the wing clipped budgies and let them walk along his fingers and he'd whistle and talk to them.

This went on week after week under Pompey's watchful gaze, till one particular Sunday Dad dozed off in his arm chair, relaxed after his beers, with his glasses slipped to the end of his nose, his false teeth half ejected from his mouth and the two helpless budgies perched on his hands that were now fallen in his lap. Pompey didn't need a second chance, Dad jolted awake to the weight of Pompey on his stomach in a billow of feathers, but it was too late to save Paddy and Polly.

In the back door to the kitchen, I could hear

John Holt singing Mr. Bojangles from the living-room stereo. There was no evidence of a dinner on, which reminded me Dad was working. *It must be Jackie home early.* I opened the living room door increasing the volume of music and babblings of conversation, to see Shane with about eight others, all in school uniform, three of which were girls. I fanned my hand in front of my face as cigarette smoke stung my nostrils. They stopped talking and looked at me as Shane reached and lowered the volume. Rising smoke from the cigarettes, some resting at-slant in saucers on the coffee table, joined the haze that waltzed across the ceiling.

"What you doing home, Ant?"

"Its home time," I said.

"Shit, c'mon you've all got to go," Shane said, as he got up and lifted the needle off the rotating vinyl, plunging the room to silence.

"Is it that time already?" one of the girls said, as she stubbed her cigarette into a saucer.

Shane looked around the room, his hands resting on the hips of his grey school trousers. "Come on lads, Jude, Sam, Tina tidy the place up a bit, empty them saucers and open the windows."

Then he looked at me. "Where's Mary Louise, Ant?"

"She's gone to Sarah's house, Sarah's nan collected them from school, and I'll collect her before dinner."

"Don't mention this to Dad, alright."

"I won't."

I stood to one side as they filed out through the hall with their school bags. I went out and checked the chickens. They had laid two eggs for me. When I got back to the kitchen Tracey and Michelle arrived in from school and they started on the kitchen straight away, Tracey started washing potatoes at the sink while Michelle placed a shoulder of bacon in to the pressure cooker to boil.

"Dad said he wants bacon, cabbage and spuds, Ant, will you go out and dig up one of Dad's cabbages?" Michelle said.

"A nice big one, Ant," Tracey ordered.

I walked through the drills of Dad's vegetable plot, with its cabbage, potatoes, tomatoes, lettuce, spring onions, sweet peas, and carrots. I dug below the root to unearth the cabbage and thought how often Dad cursed the soil *It'll grow nothing* and so he fertilized it every year with horse manure, stinking half the estate out for a day or two in the process.

Jackie came home from working in Eileen's Fashions in the city and took her usual position, with a cushion on the floor a yard away from the television and switched it to BBC 2 which would show her favourite black and white movies starring James Cagney, Spencer Tracey or James Stewart. Back in those days Jackie wouldn't accept that she was short sighted *I'm alright I just like sitting down here, that's all* she'd say when Dad suggested a visit to the optician. One day I noticed Jackie sitting back on an armchair for the first time watching a movie, it made me look twice, and it was on the second glance that I noticed she had my glasses held to her eyes.

"What you doing with my glasses Jackie? I've been looking for them everywhere."

"They're flippin great Ant, these are. I can see everything with them."

I collected Mary Louise from Sarah's, and Dad arrived home. And we all sat around the table for dinner. With bacon and cabbage on each plate we had a large bowl of potatoes in their skins in the centre of the table.

"Now use those saucers for peeling your potatoes on," Dad said. *The saucers had many uses.*

"I want to go night fishing tonight," Shane said, as he looked straight across the table at Dad.

"Where, Shane?"

"Only Shardend lake."

"Who's going with yer?"

"Tommy, Danny and Dessie."

Dad knew these were Shane's better choice of friends, and that Shane had a genuine love of fishing.

"Okay, well I might call up to yer, see how you're getting on Shane, and if I catch you drinking cider you won't be out for a month."

"I won't Dad, that was just once and it made me sick, I'm going at half past twelve, but I'm going to have three hours sleep first."

"You won't wake up Shane, you're better off staying awake or going earlier," Dad said.

"I'll be alright."

"Shane, won't the fish be asleep?" Mary Louise said, and we all laughed.

"Actually, bab, some of them do hide under logs and rest during the night but there's other fish types that are shy during the day and a lot more active at night time, you see there's no boat traffic either and then you also have the best spots to choose from with no one else around."

After dinner, the girls tidied the kitchen as Shane was going through his fishing boxes.

"Dad I'm going over to Sam's house," Jackie said.

"Nobody is going anywhere till after we've said the rosary,"

"Can we just say one decade?" Jackie said.

"No, it's the third glorious mystery, the descent of the Holy Ghost, so it's the full five then you can go to Sam's."

We all knelt on the floor around the living room leaning on arm chairs, the coffee table and the sofa as Dad got his prayer-book out and passed around our beads.

"Shane, turn around and face the Sacred Heart like the rest of us," Dad said, as Shane shifted slightly, and the prayers began.

After the Rosary, I was in the garden when Michelle came over.

"Hey Ant, have you tasted them new fizzy Bam bars in the Asian shop?"

"No."

"They're lovely but they're ten pence each and they have loads of other new stuff too, go and ask Dad for some money, he's been to work today, he'll probably give it you."

"Okay."

I went through the house to the living room where Dad was dozing in his arm chair.

"Dad, Dad."

"What do you want, son?"

"Can I have ten pence?"

"What for?"

"Sweets, Dad."

"No."

"Oh, please Dad."

"Anthony, I said no, now let me sleep."

I went back out to Michelle in the garden.

"He won't give it to me, and he's trying to sleep," Michelle smiled and said,

"Watch this."

I followed her as she walked through the house but I stayed back in the hallway and watched as she walked over to Dad in the chair.

"Dad, can I have a pound, please?"

"No, Michelle, will you let me sleep?"

"Dad, I need a pound for things, Dad, girl things."

Dad jumped up out of his chair, prodded his glasses to the top of his nose, reached into his pocket and pulled out his wallet and handed Michelle a pound note.

"Thanks Dad," she said, as he settled himself back in the chair and she turned and winked as she sauntered out towards me.

"What the hell are girl things Michelle?" I said, back in the garden.

"Nothing, Ant, it's just another way of asking, I'm off to the shop, see ya."

I stood in the garden, my hands on my hips, mulling Michelle's words over as I looked back at the house, it's sandy pebble-dash finish, the netted windows. Two small birds flew low from one side of my gaze in a playful pursuit, dipping, surging then away to the other side, drawing my eye with them. *Just another way of asking.* I went back in to Dad. I stood at the side of his arm chair; his eyes were closed.

"Dad, Dad."

"Wha-what."

His eyes opened slightly.

"Dad, can I have a pound, Dad, I need a pound for boy's things Dad?"

As I said it, I leaned forward, a little closer, imitating Michelle's movements. He turned his head towards mine his sleepy eyes shot open, his cheeks reddened.

"Anthony, will yer piss off now and let me sleep before I give you a slap?"

I left the room fast.

That night at bed time Shane joined me, it had been a while since we went to bed at the same time. Our room was at the front of the house, with two single beds at the walls under the window to the left and right. The walls that Dad painted the claret and blue of Aston Villa. With all his fishing gear ready in the hall way by the door, Shane's only concern was not waking up. I sat in my bed and watched Shane in confusion.

"What you doing Shane?"

"Des, Tom and Dan are calling around at half twelve but they can't knock the door cos they'll wake everyone up and everyone knows I'm a heavy sleeper."

"So, what are you doing with the string?"

"I'm tying it to my big toe and throwing the ball of it out the window, down to the porch door and the lads are going to wake me by pulling it."

So, Shane set about his plan and hopped in to bed and said,

"Ant, switch off the light, kid."

"Okay."

I awoke later in the night to the sound of whistles coming in through the open window, as my eyes adjusted, I reached for my glasses and held them in place. I watched as the curtain lifted over the string as it was tightening, raising Shane's foot and drawing night-light on to his bed. The blanket slipped off his bare leg and it hung there for a few seconds, his skin shining white in the moon light.

"Fuck off, fuck off," Shane said sleepily, as he was trying to pull his leg down. I could hear laughing from the lads down at the porch.

"Fuck off now," Shane said, as he tried to roll over on to his side.

His shoulders went over but his leg remained elevated in the other direction, then the string snapped and his leg fell to the bed and he pulled it in to his blanket with loose string attached and the curtain swung back to its drape, leaving the room to darkness. My heart was pumping fast as I sat up in my bed and I could hear the voices of Shane's friends fading as they walked further from the house. Conceding their first of the night, *one that got away*.

It was my desire to be good that was still guiding me on at this time, and would continue for the next few years. Though I often failed, I tried. Like I tried to live with my confusion and the void that, like a vanishing trick, left me mystified. I was still a few years away from listening to music and lyrics and discovering Bruce Springsteen, who became my therapy. Through his lyrics and my imagination, he understood me and my situation.

Especially about wanting to get the fuck out and away. Still to *this* day I get drawn back to his great archive and choose a record, the most healing for my turmoil, (of the particular moment, or not, even.) Just to my own archive of unhealed emotional scars.

APRIL 5TH 2012

Thursday brings an end to the dry spell with a storm. I run from my car to the hospital entrance, as the low, gunmetal, sky releases heavy rain, that the wind drives to diagonals. Relieved to be under cover I speak to the serious looking security guard for the first time, and he seems pleased to see me today.

"That's some change in the weather, mate."
 As I say it, I realise that I only amused him with the calamitous way in which I'd entered. I pounded up the stairs pulled at one door then pulled at the other then cursed myself for not looking up from the ground to read the PUSH sign.

"Yeah, that's our summer over now," he says smirking.

"Yeah, that could be it, mate, good luck," I say, rounding the corner, anxious to move on.
In the corridor of the Neuro Oncology Department the smell of the ethyl-alcohol sanitation mounts on the walls remind me to cleanse, so I press the heel of my hand to one near the reception and smear my hands till dry. I look through the windows of the doors to the ward and I see Annie sitting up, propped by pillows behind her so her head is set back, swan-like, the tight, white bandage a coronet-

symbol of the seriousness of this moment. Niamh and Annie are genuinely pleased to see me though, they are both smiling as I come towards the bed. Annie with colouring books and coloured pencils around her lap and looking a little healthier.

"Good morning Daddy" she says, as I lean in to kiss her.

"Morning, Annie, and good morning Mommy."

"Morning Daddy," Niamh says, still smiling up at me from her chair.

"The nurses said Annie's responding very well on all levels of her recovery."

"Oh, that's great news, brilliant, good girl Annie."

"Will you wait here Ant, while I go and get myself sorted?"

"Course. You look a bit tired."

"I'm shattered, I don't like wearing those plugs in my ears all the time in case Annie's calling me, and sometimes she does so I lie with her. But then the bloody noises keep me awake."

"I'll stay tonight, you go home to our bed."

"No, no way, I'll be fine, really, see you in a while."

She stands up and I stand in front of her and hold her arms and kiss her cheek.

"I love you, Niamh".

"I love you too, I'll be back in a bit," she whispers, her chin quivering.

I walk to the window and watch the people below hurrying in different directions, holding on to their hats and hoods, an umbrella getting turned inside out. The rain thrashes against the window in a rhythm known only to the wind. Constant beads run down the glass. I think of my mother, of her suffering in her last year. Brought home from the hospital, for they could do no more, of her *knowing* she was dying, leaving her six children behind. I think of her anniversary and this now, how they clash. My logical mind knows how similar circumstances and coincidences happen. I know that. But my heart, my desperate heart yearns for some nameless interpretation. I swipe the mist formed by my breath on the glass with the side of my hand. Yesterday evening I parked at the parish church on the way home. Inside I lit a candle from a diminished one in full glow and I watched the small flame slither down the wick, it floundered a little as it reached the wax, then flickered proudly to its *own* full glow.

"Mommy, watch over us now and please help Annie."
With my own words spoken aloud and the acoustic of the church seeming to increase them, I felt embarrassed and looked over both shoulders to make sure I was alone. I said a silent prayer, blessed myself and left.

I sit down beside Annie and watch her as she colours in a flower. Lailani comes over and I shift my chair to give her room. She gently removes the drip feed from Annie's hand and reassures her that this is a big part of getting better.

"Daddy," Lailani says, looking at me with her brows high, her slack forehead darkened, rubbing Annie's hand.

"When Annie wants to go to the toilet next time, I think it's okay for her to try and walk, holding on to yourself or Mommy of course."

"Oh, okay very good, thank you nurse."

"No problem," she says wheeling the drip machine away from the bed.

Niamh returns looking fresh, her dark brown hair is damp and tied back in a ponytail.

"How are you feeling?"

"Better, I had cereal, fruit and yogurt and it done the job."

"Lailani said Annie can walk to the loo next time with one of us and she's removed the drip."

"Oh, I didn't even notice, well that's great progress Annie."

Niamh places Annie's thin hand in to her palm, a miniature version of her own, and gently rubs the back where the drip penetrated.

A while later as I sit reading a newspaper and Niamh is texting her sisters, Annie says.

"Mommy, I need a wee-wee."

Gently, we sit her on the side of the bed and put her slippers on, then with my hand under her arm I take some of her weight as she eases down till her feet touch the floor and she stands there for a moment.

"Maybe we should have done a trial run, I mean, are you bursting to go? What if you do a wee-wee half way across the floor?" I say,

Annie leans back on to the bed laughing.

"Daddy don't say that."

And we all laugh together. She straightens up again and with small steps we slowly get across the floor and out to the hallway, where Niamh takes her into the toilets. On the return journey through the hallway a small crowd of seven or eight doctors and nurses gather and watch Annie as she takes short steps with just her hand linking my arm, when we make it to the bed, they give a few claps, with praises of, "well done," "good girl," and "you're mighty."

It feels good to have something to smile about, something small but positive to share in our replies to the calls and texts.

It is early afternoon when Dr Timmins strolls in to the ward and stands over Annie's bed, dressed in full green surgery garb, a face mask pulled down around his neck.

"Hello Annie, Anthony and Niamh good afternoon."

"Good afternoon doctor," Niamh says.

"Good afternoon Mark, er, Doctor," I say.

I notice Niamh feels as nervous around the doctor as I do, I put my hand out to shake his and as he takes it and smiles as I do this I realise the hand shaking is unnecessary.

"How are you feeling Annie?" he says, looking down at her.

"I'm good."

"Have the headaches gone away now?"

"Yes"

"That's good, have you not washed your lovely hair yet?"

"No."

"Wash her hair?" Niamh says.

"No, I'm only joking Niamh. What part of England is that accent from Anthony?"

"Er, Birmingham, Birmingham Doc."

"I thought so, I go over a couple of times a year to Birmingham."

"Oh yeah, to the Motor Show?"

"No, no, to the children's hospital, lectures and stuff, all work related really."

"Oh, very good, it's so handy now isn't it? A nice short flight," I say.

"Oh yes, very. How about you Niamh, what part of the country are you from?"

"Mayo, Doctor, north west Mayo and it's more like a good four-hour drive home for me unfortunately."

Has he got bad news for us? Is this is his way of building up to it.

"Oh Mayo, a lovely county. I was in Westport a few times, great town."

"Yes, we were married in Westport," Niamh says.

"Very good, very good," Mark says, as he clasps his hands together and looks back at Annie.

"Has Annie done any walking yet?"

"Yes, she walked to the bathroom with Anthony earlier."

"That's good, encourage that and try to do a bit more each time, and if she wants to try something else encourage that too. Children recover quickly, unlike us, as they do far less thinking about it."

"Okay, will do doctor, er, Doctor is there a date on when we will get results on the other thing?" Niamh asks.

"Well, it has been sent to the lab and I don't know how busy they are, but I would say it will be after the long weekend now at this stage."

"Okay, doctor," Niamh says.

"I'll talk to you again, bye Annie."

With a smile he turns and takes long strides out of the ward.

"I never know what to say to him, Niamh, I mean I hold him in such high regard that I get nervous and uneasy with him."

"I know, I'm a bit like that too, it's like I'm in awe of him for what he's done."

"Yeah, exactly."

"But, *the Motor Show*, what were you thinking."

"I know, I'm such an idiot."

"It's going to be a long Easter weekend, waiting on these results."

"I know and it won't be first thing Tuesday either, I wouldn't imagine."

"Oh, what's this?" Niamh says.

I look up to see Mags and Lailani coming through the ward doors with a large, tan teddy bear and a pink love heart balloon tied to the arm, with, *get well soon Annie* printed across. Petite Lailani can barely be seen behind the teddy. Mags pulls the string of the balloon down to stop it catching on the ceiling lights. Annie sits up-right in the bed, her eyes widening and she starts to smile as she reads the message on the balloon.

"Get well soon Annie, oh Mommy who is it off?"

And she holds her arms out to receive the teddy from Lailani, and squeezes it on to herself. Its mass obscuring her momentarily, till she appears over its shoulder with a broad smile.

"It's so soft Mommy."

Niamh takes a large envelope off Mags and opens it. There's twenty-seven coloured messages in Irish with pictures drawn below them, the authors and artists being each member of her class, and a greeting card with, *Get well soon Annie, from the parents of your class mates and teachers.*

"What are you going to call your teddy, Annie?" I say,

Annie tries to wrestle the teddy to one side to read the messages off her class mates. She is overcome with excitement.

"Oh, er, his name is Ginger, Daddy. Yes, its Ginger the bear, and he's so cuddly."

"Ahh, very good Annie, great name," Mags says, as she stands at the foot of the bed with Lailani. The two nurses smiling at the sight of a child in good spirits.

Annie remains that way for the rest of the evening

as she proudly shows us each individual message from her classmates and translates them for me.

"Look Daddy, some of these boys I've never even spoke to before."

It's a great move by the teachers and parents and it gives Niamh and I the pleasure of seeing Annie in her best form for a while.

It's late evening as we sit around her bed while she sleeps, replying to the texts that are flooding our phones.

I stand from my chair, stretch and walk to the window to see that the storm has passed and I watch the darkness descend over Temple Street sooner this evening than the previous, the street lights shimmering on the wet pavement. I look across to the tall spire of St George's Church, silhouetted and featureless against a dark grey sky. A random shudder of my shoulders and vertebrae makes me appreciate the heat in the ward.

"Anthony, look, Marie's doing her rounds," Niamh whispers. So, I sit back beside her and watch as the therapist speaks with the parents on the ward.

"I think she enjoys my stories Niamh."

"Well let's face it, you don't leave her much choice."

"Well, she keeps coming back doesn't she?"

"Ant, that's her job."

"Sshh, she's coming over."

"You're such an eejit."

"Hello guys," Marie says, as she pulls up a chair. "I'm hearing good things about Annie from the nurse, oh God help us, will you look at the size of that teddy bear, where did that come from?"

"The parents and teachers at her school clubbed together," Niamh says.

"I'd say she was delighted, was she?"

"Oh, she was over the moon, especially with the messages and sketches she got off each of her class mates."

"Oh, did she? Very good, and you both seem little happier yourselves this evening."

"Well, it's been our best day of the week. She walked with me to the bathroom," I say.

"Yes, I heard that, Mags was telling me so, well that's great progress."

"And we managed to get out for lunch together, earlier this afternoon while Annie was taken for a scan," I tell her.

"Oh that was nice, because its important in difficult circumstances that you try and spend a little time together if possible, although I understand it's not easy to do so."

"Yeah, I find it helps to talk," I say, as Niamh reaches over and holds my hand.

"How did you two come to meet? Anthony, you being from Birmingham and all?"

"Well, Niamh's from the same village as my mother was from in Mayo."

"Oh right."

"Yeah, and I used to come over on holidays. I would stay with my aunt and it was one such trip over the new year that we struck up a friendship."

"What, a holiday romance, was it?"

"Well, yes and no, I actually hadn't planned on staying around you see, it was an accident as such."

WEDNESDAY JANUARY 3rd 1996

I was pleased to see the sign WELCOME TO COUNTY DUBLIN. I'd been driving almost four hours from Rossport and the last hour was in darkness with only street lights in the towns of Enfield and Kinnegad, the rest was black darkness beyond the headlights. The wind was picking up and I could feel the gusts shake my van on exposed parts of the road. I was looking forward to getting into Dublin port and settling down on the ferry with a feed and a drink in a comfortable corner where I could sleep 'til we reached Holyhead in the morning.

I rounded the bend at Heuston station and on to the quays, where the fine buildings gave me shelter from the gusts, and the roads were well-lit. The build-up of traffic with the changing lights at junctions allowed me time to take in the surroundings as I approached O'Connell Bridge, the hub of this historic city. The fluorescent buildings and tall street-lights that crook at the lamp, sent bright streaks reflecting on the dancing black waters all along the River Liffey, giving a twofold illusion.

The traffic lights changed to green and a tall, lit monument stole my eye to the right but I had to follow the signage to Dublin port. *I must pay this city a proper visit sometime. A weekend over with the lads for a drinking session, and a little look around.* With the east of the city on the sea front I was in Dublin port in five minutes. There I followed the signs for my ferry, driving parallel to tram tracks between large stacks of steel containers and crane jibs thrusting into the night sky. With only an hour and a half before sailing it seemed quiet. *Maybe I'm a little early and the big rush will start soon, maybe I misread my ticket and I've missed the ferry.*

I approached a barrier in the road but couldn't see any one around so I switched the light on in my van and checked my ticket times, I was correct, it was scheduled to sail in an hour and a half, at eight thirty. I jumped with fright as a face appeared at my driver window, a uniformed man holding his hat with his hand. I lowered my window and a gust of wind hit my face and lifted my mop of curly hair.

"Are you alright Bud?" he said.

"Er, yeah I'm supposed to be getting the eight thirty sailing to Holyhead, Mate."

"I don't think so bud, all the ferries are cancelled due to this bleedin' gale force wind."

"Fuck, er sorry, I mean, are you sure, Mate?"

"I'm positive, it's been on the RTE news and all."

"Well, when's the next sailing?"

"Well, this is it ye see, it's giving high winds for the rest of the week."

"Shit, I'm meant to be back to work on Friday."

"Are you a Brummie?"

"Yeah."

"Listen Brum, just keep calling the number on your ticket, you might get lucky."

"Okay, Mate, thanks."

"Good luck, Brum."

I turned my van around and drove slowly out through the port as I processed the situation. *I need to get home, this holiday is well and truly over, my work, my life is all in Birmingham, I need a phone box, I'll call Dad he'll get word to my work mates that I'm stranded for a day or two, it might die down tomorrow, I'll get a bed and breakfast somewhere.* I drove back into the city and parked on Aston Quay, and walked across O'Connell Bridge where I could see a phone box and I could also see the tall, lit monument that stole my eye and I smiled that my return came a lot sooner than expected. I thought of an uncle I have living in Dublin somewhere, Uncle Michael my mother's brother. He lived in Birmingham for five years. He stayed at our house at weekends when my mother was alive. I met him over a year ago in Rossport at my Granny's funeral and he remained true to my childhood memory, a gentleman. In the phone box I called Dad twice but it just rang out, so I tried Tracey.

"Trace, I'm stranded in Dublin for a day or so, all the ferries are cancelled due to gale force winds."

"And have yer got money for a BnB or something?"

"Yeah, but I'm not loaded after Christmas and

all that. The bloke I spoke to in the port said its promised high winds for the week."

"You could really do without that, Ant."

"Tell me about it. Tell dad to get word to Tommy and Eddie that I'm gonna be a few days late for work, hopefully I'll be back in time to start on Monday now."

"Okay, why don't you look up uncle Michael, Ant?"

"Yeah, I was thinking that myself, has Dad got a contact number for him?"

"I think he has, I'll nip down to Dad's house and get it for ya."

"Sound, thanks Trace, I'll call back from this phone box in about an hour."

"Okay, talk then."

I checked the time and strolled into the Bachelor's Inn pub and ordered a Guinness. I sat in a high stool at the bar and read quotes and lines from all the great Irish writers of the past that adorned the walls while my Guinness was settling. As I took my first sip, I decided I wouldn't have more than one while I still had driving to do. I pondered my situation, it was an awkward one, one I wasn't familiar with, but I knew I'd get through it, I couldn't be the first person to have to make a pint of Guinness last an hour. After fifty minutes, I called Tracey who provided me with a contact number for Uncle Michael, it rang out the first time, but on the second time trying, it answered.

"Hello."

"Hello, is that Michael Burke?"

"It is, yes."

"Mick, it's Anthony Giblin."

"Oh, how you doing Anthony? Good to hear from you."

"Mick, I'm stranded in Dublin, I'm meant to be sailing to Holyhead tonight but all ferries are cancelled due to the wind and I'm told it could be a few days before the wind dies down and I'm wondering if you could put me up for a night or two?"

"Sure Anthony, I have a bed here you can use, no problem at all. So where are you now?"

"I'm in a phone box near O'Connell Bridge, Mick."

"Oh, well I'm only up the road from you, it's called Dorset street, I'm near a pub called Mayes I can meet you there if you like? Will I give you directions?"

"No, Mick, Mayes Pub, Dorset Street, that's fine see you soon."

Mick was right, he was only up the road, on the North-side, a ten-minute walk, in fact. But my van was parked on the south side of the river on a one-way system, and my pronunciation of Dorset street to a stationary taxi driver, beside my van, was mistaken for Dawson Street. And so, I began my discovery of South-Side inner-city Dublin and its one-way roads. It was on my third lap of St

Stephens Green that I decided to park up and get out. I approached a middle-aged man walking and asked for directions to Mayes Pub on Dorset Street.

"Ahh Jasus. Dat's way over on the north side, you've got to get on to the North Circular Road and it's just off dat."

"Well, I've been on the south circular road twice, are they connected?"

"No. You've got to cross over the river."

"Oh, oh yes, the fucking river splits the city, that's where I'm going wrong. I know the South Side like the back of my hand now, now I know where I'm going wrong. Thanks mate."

By the time I parked up near Mayes Pub on Dorset Street, I just wanted to put the day behind me.

I pulled the heavy door, releasing lively talk and laughter from groups of men around the tables and bar. The walls and shelves were decorated in GAA memorabilia of county badges and flags, smoke lingered and swirled at the ceiling lights. I spotted Mick on a high stool at the far end of the bar. His broad shoulders, wavy hair and glasses the way I recalled. He saw me, and hoisted his hand with raised fore-finger.

"How 'yer getting on, Anthony? I was beginning to think you changed your mind."

We shook hands, smiling, as our eyes examined each other's familiar features.

"No, I just had a little trouble finding the place that's all."

"What yer having?"

"Guinness please, Mick."

"Two pints of Guinness there Pat, good man."

I awoke in the morning to the sound of traffic on Dorset Street, the sequence of traffic lights determining the revving of engines as they change. I remembered waking in the night and stumbling across the floor of Mick's flat searching for the bathroom to piss, and I saw Mick asleep on his couch in his living/kitchen room and realised the bed he gave me was his own. I went to the window to check the weather, and saw my contact lenses in their case on the sill and placed them in with rehearsed precision. The morning was bright and wet, I searched the street from the first storey window for a sign of wind. The roads were heavy with traffic and the street had more pubs than shops. Commuters hurried about on their busy way, wearing overcoats and scarves. I noticed a tricolour was hanging outside Flannigan's Bar frantically flapping in the wind. The smell of breakfast coming from the other room evoked a hunger in me. I got dressed and followed my nose.

"Good morning Anthony." Mick said, as he turned sausages on the sizzling pan.

"Morning Mick."

"Did you sleep well?"

"I did, but if I knew you were gonna be on the small couch here, I wouldn't have took your bed."

"Oh, don't worry about that, I often sleep on that couch there when I have drink on me. Do you like sausage, bacon and eggs?"

"Oh, yes please."

"That's good, there's a newspaper over there on the table if you want to read it. I was across at the shop and the wind is no better than yesterday."

"Yeah, I looked out and seen a flag blowing wild. I'll ring the port to confirm after breakfast."

After eating. I stood up from the table and rinsed my plate in the sink.

"Don't worry about that Anthony, sit down."

I sat in an armchair and looked around the cosy living / kitchen room with its bathroom at one end and the bedroom to the other.

"Thanks a lot for this Mick."

"Ahh, no bother at all, its seldom I do get visitors. You're certainly a birthday present I wasn't expecting."

"When's your birthday Mick?"

"Yesterday."

"Oh, happy birthday for yesterday Mick, ha-ha, nice one. Right, I'm gonna call Dublin port and see if there's any sailings."

"The phone out in the hall way there, takes ten pence pieces. I have a few if you need them."

"I'm okay, I've got plenty of change from the bar last night."

In the hallway on the residents phone it only cost me ten pence to learn all ferries remained cancelled due to severe gale-force winds. So, I rang Dad.

"Alright Dad?"

"Alright son, how yer getting on? I heard you're stranded for a few days, did yer find Michael?"

"Yeah, I'm at his place now, I'm fine, just a bit pissed off, will you get word to Tommy and Eddie today? 'Cos they started back yesterday and I was due back in on Friday."

"I will son, of course, don't worry about it. There's nothing you can do but wait it out and we'll see you in a few days, please God. How you fixed for shillings?"

"I'm okay Dad, I got a few quid in the bank still."

"Good lad. Okay Anthony we'll talk tomorrow."

"Bye Dad."

I sat in the armchair drinking tea as Mick came out from shaving in the bathroom, he sat down on the couch.

"I didn't get talking right to you last night, what with the excitement of your evening and all. How's all the family at home? Who's living at home with your father now?"

"Well, they're all good Mick, it's just me, living with Dad when I'm not working out of town. Jackie, Michelle and Tracey all have kids now and live in their own places around the area, Mary Louise did well at school and stayed on an extra year, she got a few O levels. Then she decided to move to Mayo, to be close to Roseleen, and she's working in Bellmullet for now."

"That's right, I heard from Rose she was over alright, and what's Shane up to?"

"Shane's his own man Mick, ducking and diving, living each day like it's his last."

"He was that way surely, even back when I

99

knew him."

"But he's not a bad bloke, Mick. Actually, he's a well-liked character around the place, the likable fool type."

"I know, I know what yer mean, no badness in him, I'd say he's decent behind it all."

"Yeah, then there's Dad himself, he hasn't changed a bit, he just struggles on throughout it all, still trying to correct our Shane with wasted words of wisdom."

I stood up from the armchair and stretched myself with raised arms and spread fingers, as I tried to talk while yawning.

"Yer know Mick, I think...yaaaaaaaah...I think that bacon has made me thirsty so I'm gonna freshen up and quench it in one of the many bars that I see on this Dorset Street."

"Well, I'll have to come with yer, to make sure you don't get lost again."

Michael was the second youngest of Anthony and Mary Burke's seven children, and with my mother being the youngest they were quite close growing up. In 1961 Michael answered the call to London where his older brother Tom fixed him up with work in construction. He lived there for fifteen years, then moved up to Birmingham where he worked and settled, till my mother died. Dublin has been his home since. It was a little after one in the afternoon when we pulled out two high stools at the bar and sat in silence as we observed the first of our pints poured to perfection. Excitable, bouncing waves of cream that coalesced to a black tranquility, with a level, creamy summit that settled taller than the glass, and curved a small perfect arc to meet it. It took a few before we got talking again.

"How was your holiday in Rossport anyway?"

"It was good, Mick, I was out with Jimmy a few times in the local and I was in Bellmullet a few nights with Mary Louise and I, er … got friendly with a local Rossport girl, Niamh McGrath, I met her last time I was over too and we've kind of kept in touch a little bit, but it's just harmless really."

"Oh, I know the McGrath family. You seem to enjoy your holidays to Rossport don't you? I mean, there's *not* a lot for a young man like yourself to do really."

"Well, I know what yer mean, but I *do* enjoy them all the same. I keep busy with Jimmy when the weather is good to work out-side. I've been coming twice a year now for the past three years, I…I kind of feel closer to my mother in a way, if I'm honest."

"How's the work going for yer beyond?"

"Oh, great Mick, I've never been out of work since I left school. I thought I'd just do a bit of construction for a while till I'd get driving lessons paid for and buy a car. But then I started to take an interest, and I'm self-employed now, and it's taken me around a few places like London, Manchester, Wales and I worked a few months in Germany. And getting out and about I suppose added to the attraction for me. But I'm back in Brum now and I've got plenty on. And Dad and myself get on well around the house."

"Do you have a girlfriend at home or do you bother at all?"

"Oh, I do bother Mick, ha-ha. But er, well I've had a few girlfriends but nothing that's lasted long, I don't think I know how to hold down a relationship or maybe I'm holding back. I don't know, maybe I'm a bit lost. Nothing's worked out so far anyway."

"Well, I can't give you any advice there because I haven't been too successful with them *myself* down the years. But sure, you're only a young man yet, what age are you now anyway?"

"Twenty-four last month."

"Jesus Christ, aren't the years flying? Two pints of Guinness there Pat."

"Mick, I'll sleep on the couch tonight no problem."

"No, you won't, you can have the bed. I'll stay with Betty tonight."

"Who's Betty?"

"Betty lives on the floor above me, I stay up there sometimes. She's someone I got friendly with but it's harmless really."

"Good one."

I awoke the following morning and checked the weather at the window straight away. It was a dull grey sky, but dry, and Flannigan's flapping flag told me there was no let-up in the wind. But I called the port anyway, no sailing. I made tea and sat in the armchair, pondering. Then Mick entered.

"Morning."

"Good morning, another windy one, did yer call?"

"Yeah, still no sailing."

"Are you hungry? I'll get the breakfast on."

"That'll be nice, thanks."

After breakfast we sat drinking tea when he said. "You seem fed up today."

"I am Mick, I just want to get back now. I want to get back to work and get in to my routine again."

"Well, there's plenty of work here now yer know."

"What?"

"And there's talk of a building boom starting."

"What are you saying?"

"Well sure, you're self-employed, you have no ties at home, there's work here and more promised, and sure don't you have a woman here now as well."

I took the cup away from my mouth and sat bolt up-right as tea ran down my chin, I swallowed then laughed. Mick smiled as he passed me a kitchen towel.

"No Mick, that's crazy, that's just crazy. I live with Dad and we're like best mates, and I have work at home and Niamh's not my woman, it's just a holiday romance thing or whatever and we both accept it as that."

"Well, you could do a lot worse."

"No, sorry, it's not an option."

"They say everything happens for a reason Anthony, but sure I don't know."

"Do you want anything from the shop? I'm going for a walk. I need to clear my head."

"Get me a paper, will you? Good man, there's change on the table there."

"I'm okay."

I put on my jacket and walked to the corner at Maye's pub. I raised my collars and pulled them together and held them under my chin as I turned on to Frederick Street, in to the strong wind. I arrived on Parnell Square and the Garden of Remembrance. There I turned and descended the steps into the attractive indent of landscape that forms the garden, and I mulled over Mick's words as I walked the path around the large cross shaped pool of water. *I know Mick has a point; he has a very good point.*

I thought of a conversation I had with a man the week before in Rossport, in the pub. He told me he only recently moved back home again to retire, he had lived and worked in London since he was a young man. He said he went to school with my mother and that he remembered travelling up to Birmingham with others for her funeral. We spoke about work, as he was at the same line of work as myself. He mentioned how he was offered work recently in Dublin but turned it down, he handed me the builder's business card which I put in my wallet along with others.

I stood watching the shallow pool for a while, as it rippled and swayed in the wind like a current. And I smiled as I thought of Niamh, a sweet nineteen-year-old country girl doing a computer course in Galway somewhere. *Does she really need someone like me in her life, with my baggage, my lack of direction. Does she even want it? That will be the decider for me, fuck it, I've got nothing to lose.* I walked back up Frederick Street with butterflies in my stomach and the wind at my back, and I found a phone box on Dorset street. I wanted to call the number I had for Niamh first, but I couldn't bring myself to do it. I opened my wallet and took out the recent inclusion to my collection of contractor's cards.

Doherty Contractor's, Castleknock, Dublin, specialists in reinforced concrete structures.

"Hello, is this Doherty contractors?"

"Yes, this is Tony Doherty, who's speaking?"

"Hello Tony, my name's Anthony Giblin, I do shuttering and steel fixing and I was wondering if you're taking any men on?"

"I would be looking for steel fixers alright, they're like hen's teeth at the moment, are you at it long, I mean, can you read the drawings and all?"

"Oh yeah, I have no problems there."

"Okay, let me see, you don't sound too local, do you know Blanchardstown at all?"

"Well, I'm from Birmingham, but I'm here in Dublin and I have a van with me, so I'll find it."

"Oh, you're grand so, well I tell yer, I have good news and bad news, the good is, I'll start yer no problem, I pay the rate around the town at the moment but if you're competent with the drawings I'll look after you. Now the problem is I won't have anything for a week cos this fucking storm is affecting all the tower cranes in the town, so we're experiencing a bad start to the year. Will you call me in four days' time, Anthony? And we'll take it from there."

"I will, no problem, thank you."

"Good luck."

"Bye."

My excitement grew. *One box ticked, I've gotta keep going, I'm on a roll here.* I dialled a number Niamh gave me for her college, she told me to only use it if I really had to.

I was put on hold till she was brought to the phone.

"Hello."

"Hello Niamh, it's Anthony."

"Anthony, what are you doing calling me here? Did you get home okay?"

"No Niamh, and that's why I'm calling, are you okay to talk?"

"Yeah, yeah, what's wrong?"

"Well, there's been no sailing due to the gale-force winds so I'm in Dublin here and I'm staying with my uncle Mick."

"Oh my god, that's unfortunate, but you're lucky to have him I suppose and, so what are you thinking?"

"Well, I'm thinking of waiting in this country for a while, I mean, I've just rang a bloke, he's a contractor and he has a job for me and well, I was I suppose I was wondering if I have a girlfriend?"

"Ha-ha-ha, you're crazy Anthony Giblin, you don't hang around, do you? When do you start work?"

"Well, this is it you see, its delayed due to the damn wind affecting the cranes also, so it won't be for a few days and I'm at a bit of a loose end here till I sort out accommodation and stuff,"

"Well, let me see, I'm sharing a cottage here in Spiddal with a girl from home and she hasn't come back since before Christmas. I called her yesterday to see what's going on and she's sick with a chest infection. So, Anthony Giblin, you better get in your van and head for Galway while I still have the place to myself."

"I'll see you in a few hours."

I'd placed the phone and made a triumphant punch in the air just as I noticed the queue of three people waiting to use the phone. When uncle Mick answered his door, he looked at me, then smiled.

"You seem a lot happier than when you left."

"That's cos I am Mick."

"Look Anthony, sorry, don't mind me, I shouldn't be telling you your business, you do your own thing. What do I know anyway?"

"No, no, I took your advice."

I handed him his newspaper as he sat back on his couch, and he just looked at me, as I went down to the bedroom and put a few belongings in to my bag, zipped it up and returned with it on my shoulder.

"I have a job with Doherty contractors, I start in Blanchardstown next week and now I'm heading for a place called Spiddal in County Galway to spend a few days with my woman."

"Good man, Jesus, you're crazy Anthony Giblin yer know that? Ha-ha."

"I know, you're the second person to tell me that today. Thanks for everything and I'll see you in a few days."

AN SPIDEAL

I made it to Galway in just under three hours, where I refuelled and reviewed my map. It surprised me the amount of country still west of Galway City. I was heading for Barna and I would call Niamh there for directions. Narrow roads with borders of thistles, nettles and gorse soon turned to narrow lanes, with margins of stone walls that were barely high enough to shield the van from the exposure of the gusts that blew in from the Atlantic Ocean, out to my left. I passed old cottage ruins with their prominent stone gables and collapsed roofs, homes of past generations. The road ascended in front of me and I looked around at fields, of varying shades of green, divided by stone walls. Stones and boulders removed from the land manually, and arranged as boundaries. Perceptible requirements of by-gone days. *I hope when I call Niamh for the final directions, she doesn't give me a land mark made of stone.* I stopped at a shop/post office and used a public phone.

"You'll see me Anthony, I'm ten minutes outside of Barna on the Spiddal road, there's cottages on the right of the road, and I'll see your van in good time, so I'll be waving outside one of them." And so she was, hands and hair waving in the wind and a big smile, as she dropped her arms and directed me in to the gravel drive way of the small white cottage. When I stepped out of the van, I felt the impact of the wind on my face, then the force of Niamh around my neck as her face shielded mine with a kiss and we remained that way, unfazed by the wind, the wind that brought me there.

It only took me a few months to realise I had hit the jackpot with Niamh. Things were finally going my way. I played ball, I didn't want to fuck it up, but I was conscious of getting too serious, too soon. After a few weeks I asked her. "What if I don't settle here, long term?" She didn't hesitate. "Well, I'm going wherever you go." I rented a room in a house in Lucan, I shared the facilities with a few decent lads of various trades. We all became friends. Taking Niamh's age in to consideration, and my own frame of mind. I made an arrangement where we would meet up only every second weekend and this suited us both. It was about as serious as I wanted to get at that time.

So, I would be on the beer in Dublin every second weekend and on the beer with Niamh in Galway every other. And working like a lunatic on sites in Dublin in between. After two years that arrangement ended when Niamh, sensing my fear of commitment and growing contentment for both worlds, got a job with a bank in Baggot Street, Dublin and moved up. She stood in front of me in my room, arms folded. "We're going to get our own place, Anthony Giblin, we're going to rent a cheap flat and save for a house." Her haste surprised me, but I knew I needed the kick up the hole.

We moved in to a small flat in Chapelizod on the fourth floor of an old building of nine flats. Alongside was a similar building, but it was neglected and disused, except for pigeons. The landlord, once he was happy with us and our deposit, allowed us to cheaply furnish the flat, complete with new carpet, bed and appliances, and deducted it from his rent when we produced receipts. It was strange at first seeing so much of each other. We quarrelled over how things should be, where they might go, how we would finance things, then we laughed about ourselves, then quarrelled again to prove we weren't giving in. After a month or so we learned how to live closely with another. With each other. We painted the four small rooms, bedroom, bathroom, kitchen, living-room. Just another wood-chip lick and put up a few posters to humour the tightness of space, Abbey road, Construction workers lunch-atop a New York skyscraper, Van the man, Springsteen and Dylan.

The cheap rent allowed us to save as house prices were creeping up. The Celtic Tiger wasn't entirely up on all fours just yet, but her hindlegs were straightening and soon she would roar.

The construction of an apartment complex in the village beside the River Liffey, seemingly upset a lot of settled rats and some decided to move in next door with the pigeons, (according to some of our neighbours below us). We went to a house party with friends in Lucan after the pub one Saturday night, it carried on in the local pub again the next morning till late evening when eventually we all drifted off to our homes and beds exhausted. My hangover at work the next morning soon turned to *the fear* by the afternoon, and I knew it would be a rough night in bed. So, I minimised my sleeping time by reading *Howard Marks, Mr. Nice* under the lamp light with Niamh sleeping beside me.

Over the top right corner of the paper back in the near distance, I thought I saw something moving, but then I would, I was in the horrors. But that still didn't convince. My heart was now thumping harder and louder. There it was again, this time I saw a hefty, long tailed rat, two yards away, scurrying across the bed-room carpet into the bathroom and out of sight. I never had a fear of rats before this moment and I never reacted the way I did either, before this moment. It was exactly the way Laurel or Hardy would when in an over dramatized mock fright. I dropped the book and leapt, standing up on my pillow with my back at the wall in stunned, dry mouthed silence. I imagine my eyes were bulging out of their sockets. Eventually words came out slowly. That woke Niamh and she joined me up on the pillow thinking it was something far, far more sinister, and *her* eyes were bulging out of their sockets. Its appearance amongst our belongings, on the new carpet, in our fairly hygienic conditions suggested we were only camouflaging an old shit hole. A pest control guy arrived the next evening and laid poison all over the building and discovered a hole behind our bathroom sink, that I filled.

A few residents got cats, we got plug in repellers, six of them. We never had another sighting but we could hear them in the walls and floors at night for a few weeks after, then nothing. But the damage was done and we both have the fear of them to this day.

It was 1998 and a great time to buy property in Ireland, especially Leinster. Ten percent of the asking price was needed as deposit, and a three-bed semi could be got for £100/120k. So, we had a target. We saved religiously, I took a supervisor role on site that I previously turned down and worked my Saturdays too. Then what happened over the coming years was common all over the capital for potential house buyers. We were chasing the increasing ten percent, as the house prices got higher. We met and spoke with similar couples at the many viewings, and got to know a few of those who had the same locations as ourselves in mind. If a couple made a bid for £185k, £5k over the asking price, it was guaranteed they would hear back in a day or two that they were in a bidding war and the mysterious bidder was always a determined fucker for a while, who would lose interest in the bid when the price went £25k over and the couple would be told their new bid was accepted.

And they wouldn't know whether to laugh or cry.

Throughout these times I purchased a Guitar and tried to learn *how to make her talk* so I could maybe put music to the song writing and poetry that I kept a secret from everyone except Niamh. I rasped chords, broke strings and pissed Niamh and the neighbours off with crazy strumming patterns. I managed to get up to a level of being crap, and gradually accepted that was my standard. My purchase was a neat, steel stringed Washburn that has never *talked*. It sits in its case all these years later in my home, under the stairs, as I imagine, like a feather-less peacock.

After the first year in the flat, naturally, the teasing hints at marriage were put to us by close friends and family. But I had convinced Niamh that marriage wasn't for me, although the opposite was true, I really had her convinced. "Anthony doesn't think marriage is important, hardly anyone gets married anymore where he's from," she'd say, seeming fine with it. And by the time we were over five years together, and still no proposal, I think I had most of the rest convinced too. But this did come back to drown me in a veil of bluffers comeuppance for a long awkward moment in The Great Southern hotel overlooking Eyre Square County Galway.

JUNE 2001

I looked out at the dull overcast morning, then down at the little Toyota Dyna pickup from the kitchen window of the flat. *How am going to do this? How the fuck am I going to get her to Galway without her guessing?* I looked at the sand in the back of the pickup. *I should have got him to empty the fucking thing.* I borrowed the pickup off a builder friend to get us to and from Galway so I could propose to Niamh in the Great Southern Hotel where I had two nights, bed, breakfast and evening meal booked since January. We both relied on public transport to get to work, this suited me while I was trying to gather money for a house and secretly, a wedding. Behind the seats of the cab was a holdall with clothes and bits and pieces for both of us that she was unaware of.

"Why couldn't we just go home to Mayo, this is shite. Everyone is home this bank holiday weekend and sure it'll be mighty craic?" Niamh said walking in to the kitchen.

"Because we do that all the time, I just want a holiday weekend where we can go places we haven't been before, Malahide, Howth, down to Wicklow."

"In a fucking pickup full of sand?"

"I got it for nothing, it's the best I could do. Come on I'll take you for a spin, it's actually more comfortable than you think."

"I'm not ready or anything, sure look at the state of me."

"You're fine." I lied, as I looked down at her in cream tattered flats, bare white skinny legs, a short flarey red skirt with an old white blouse. Her hair was loosely tied and she had her glasses on. *Shit, I must bring her contact lenses.*

"Come on, a quick spin."

"Okay, we need to get milk anyway."

And that was the first stage done. I had got her in to the pickup, and I just drove to Galway city. Niamh is a bright girl but she never copped on to my plan, she was far too angry to think.

"Where the fuck are you driving to? Take me back, NOW!"

"I don't know, we could keep going to Galway for the craic. Come on, some of the best times happen on the spur of the moment."

"Oh my God. You are *so* dead."

"If you kill me, I'll crash."

"You think this is funny? Your crazy, you know that? Absolutely fucking nuts. I'm not talking to you. When you're done spinning around the country wake me up."

She lay on her side on the double seat with her arse over beside me. I laughed and slapped it.

"Fuck off."

We arrived in Galway as a shower of rain passed

116

over and the sunshine dazzled on the wet road. I parked just off Eyre Square, I switched off the engine and woke her. She sat up and put her glasses on and wiped the back of her hand across her mouth. A line of the seat stitching made its imprint on her cheek. She was frowning at me.

"You really did it, I can't believe you. You can be so selfish sometimes. Look at the state of me."

"You look fine. Listen, we'll get something to eat and I'll drive back." I kissed her on the cheek.

"Okay, I'm starved. But I'm still mad at you."

I walked in the direction of the hotel, across the wet grass of the Square, between a few young trees with trembling leaves glinting light. She tailed me by a few yards. I knew I had to keep a pace-on to stay in charge.

"Slow down, why are we on the grass? My shoes are soaked. Where are we eating?"

"Let's try this place."

"No way, that'll cost a fortune."

I leapt up the steps of the hotel and in to the reception, she caught up with me, but only to get me out. She was pulling my sleeve hard.

"Hi, my name's Anthony Giblin, I have a double room booked for two nights with breakfast and evening meal," I said to the redhaired receptionist. Niamh's mouth fell, and her hand dropped from my sleeve. I knew I had to act fast.

"Look, just a little surprise, for a change," I said quietly. She just shook her head gently as her eyes swayed like a pendulum, searching mine. The receptionist seemed amused by us as she checked us in and a flat capped porter took us to our room over-looking the Square. Niamh went straight to the bathroom as I tipped the porter and whispered an order of a bottle of champagne (I was confident). I stood at the window looking out at the Galway Hooker fountain with its rusty metal sails.

My legs were shaking.

"Look at the state of me. Oh my God Ant, I still can't believe you've done this." She said as she emerged from the bathroom, smiling. "Come over here and have a look at this." I said pointing out of the window. As she stood beside me looking out, I lowered down on to one knee and she turned, looking down with a slight frown.

"Niamh will you marry me?"

"Oh, stop messing, that's not funny." She turned and walked four steps to the bed, they were the slowest steps I ever witnessed. She sat on the bed hunched over, removing her damp shoes. The room was quiet, but my heart was a pounding drum. She looked over at me and swept her fallen hair behind her ears and removed her glasses. Her face seemed bare; her frown deepened over her bright blue eyes as she looked in to mine. I could hear the distant rumbling of a trolley been wheeled across a floor above us. My right hand was still out to take hers. I took a knee-step forwards. "Will you marry me?" It came out in almost a whisper. "Yes, Anthony, of course I will," she shrieked.

We tried, with our romantic notions running

high, to get a house before our wedding date the following July. But reality proved far too challenging in a rising market. We returned home to the flat in wedlock, and battled on.

Fifteen months after our wedding day on a blustery October Saturday in 2003, with leaves drifting around us, we turned the key in our North Kildare home, and a small flurry of leaves entered before us.

GOOD FRIDAY 6TH APRIL 2012

Niamh asked me to be in earlier this morning. Getting in to the car I'm in good humour, this raises questions in my head. *Am I fucking detached from this situation? Is my sensitivity damaged in some way?* I drive eastwards as the morning slowly begins, the passing darkness makes way for an emergence of orange glow, that radiantly defines the undersides of the clouds over Dublin City. It's noticeably quiet on the ward, with most of the children sleeping. Niamh wants to try one of the parents resting rooms over the other end of the building, but not until I'm seated beside Annie.

"Just wait with her, I'll only be a few hours, thanks a lot."

"What are you thanking me for?"

I kiss her cheek and she tries an unconvincing smile, through her tiredness, before she turns and leaves the ward. I sit beside Annie, speed-reading through Niamh's magazines till she awakens.

"Oh, hello Daddy, where's Mommy?"

She yawns, eyes widening, fixed on the ceiling for an instant, her pale forehead creasing to the fringe of bandage, arms out-stretched. I steal the opportunity for a hug which makes her clamp her mouth shut, then laugh.

"Good morning Annie, Mommy's over at the parents' sleeping rooms, having a little rest from that floor down there."

"Okay Daddy. How's Mikey and Lukey?"

"Aahh, they're fine, they're being good boys for Nanny."

"I miss them *so* much."

"Well, maybe I can bring them in to see you tomorrow, would that be okay?"

"Oh yes, Daddy."

"Look, here's your breakfast coming."

Annie sits herself up in the bed as the porter rolls a table up to her with cereal, toast and fruit juice.

"Daddy, after breakfast will you play my arts and crafts with me, I want to make some necklaces and bracelets for the nurses."

"I'd love to."

The porter clears the cutlery around the ward, rolling the tables back to the end of the beds. Two of the other breakfasts remain untouched. Annie is bossing me with instructions as to the correct beads and bands to be used, so under her creative supervision I assemble my first necklace. A child's cry bellows down the corridor then becomes drowned by the voices of nurses and their hurried footsteps, the cry becomes a whimper, then quietness. I smile as I watch Annie's face in full concentration, her small lips pursed. Her hands and fingers working like an artisan to form a necklace and then she starts a chatter of reasoning as to why it has to be done this way. The bandaged head bowed, a healthy pink in her freckled cheeks. *I think she's going to be okay, I think she's going to be just fine. But then I didn't believe she had a tumour, what do I know? There are always hospital stories that they were great one minute and then... What if she doesn't come out of here alive? This is fucking cancer she could be up against.*

"Daddy, Daddy, you're making a mess."
I look down, I've let the beads slip through the string and roll off the bed onto the lino where they're bouncing and picking up speed and rolling in every direction.
I'm on my hands and knees making sure I've got them all when Niamh returns earlier than expected. I look up from the floor, as she stands there in trainers, leggings, t-shirt and open hoody, her hair tied back tight, and the tired look still around her eyes.

"Anthony Giblin, what are you at down there? I can't leave you alone for a minute," she says, shaking her head and glancing at one of the parents.

"I dropped a few beads and stuff, I think I got them all, how come you're back so early?"

"I couldn't sleep, I felt too far away from Annie, I felt I was missing something, my head just won't switch off, so I just showered and had a bagel."

"Well, as you can see, we've been making necklaces and stuff."

"No, Daddy, you tried to make one and I made three, he's not very good Mommy."

"Okay, good girl, now I think we'll put the arts and crafts away, Daddy help Annie put these away.

Hey, take a look who's in the corridor. It's the Doctor. Come on tidy this place up."

I put all the accessories in to little bags, separating different types, then in to the box and set it on the table at the foot of the bed just as Doctor Timmins walks around me, in his scrubs and crocs. (I heard a Doctor in the lift, referring to the garments as such.) He stands away from the bed, his back to the window, his hands by his sides, an almost military stance.

"Good morning. How is Annie today?"

"Morning Doctor," I say, as I look from him, down to Annie sitting up in the bed.

"I'm good," Annie answers shyly.

"Yeah, she seems to be improving a little every day, Doctor." Niamh says, as she fixes Annie's pillows. "We were just getting ready for a walk down the corridor."

"Very good, increase the walks for as long as she's up for it. Well, I'm pleased to tell you the test results came back benign, *and* I'm confident from the recent scan results that I got it all."

I look at the Doctor, he smiles, looking over and back from one to the other. Niamh is still leaning towards the head-board, her hands not moving as she cranes over her shoulder. I'm uncertain I heard him correctly, or I just want him to repeat his words. I look at Niamh and she stands straight and puts both hands over her mouth, and looks at me wide-eyed, slowly I take the steps towards her as I look at the Doctor and say, "You mean the tumour results are benign?"

"Yes, that's right." He smiles.

"Oh my god," Niamh says, lowering her hands from her quivering chin. "Oh my god."

I hold her. I get the sweet fragrance of her freshly washed hair, as my chest heaves and my shoulders tremble, but I'm not crying. It's not that definite. There's tears, but the guttural noise I'm making is a low laugh, and I smile with the taste of tears in my mouth. I lift my head to see Annie watching us. We step apart and both wrap our arms around Annie, and she turns to Niamh first, and my kiss misses its target as I plant it on her bandage. I turn and face the doctor as he stands tall, smiling at us. I shake his hand.

"Thank you, Doctor, thank you so much for everything you've done."

"Thanks, I'll let you have some time to yourselves," he says. Just then, Niamh asks, "Do you mind if I give you a hug?" But doesn't wait for his response as she steps up to him and puts her arms around his ribs.

"Thank you, Doctor, thank you so much," she says as her tears darken his green top. The Doctor holds his hands out, as if in surrender, then brings them down gently on Niamh's shoulders as he looks down and says, "I'll have to change again now before I go to surgery."

And we laugh together, as Annie looks on in bewilderment.

"It's all good Annie, you're going to get better

and you'll be going home," Niamh says.

Saturday night, and Niamh lets me relieve her of overnight duties, as she goes home to rest. The night blackens over Temple Street, and the lights of the ward are switched off with just the hall sending its light through the windows of the double doors. The use of bed lamps is optional. Annie and I have hers on and pointing down to her locker, where we are having a mini party, as we talk in whispers. We share Skittles, wine gums, crisps and fruit juice.

"Daddy, tell me a story."

"Which book do you want?"

"No, I want one from your head, tell me a Jimmy the Leprechaun one."

"Okay…let me see… this is called Jimmy and the sick children."

Eventually, the sugar wears off and she sleeps. It takes me a while longer, down on the foldout mattress, to one side of her. But eventually, with plugs swelled in my ears and relief in my heart, I drift off too.

Niamh arrives at midday Easter Sunday, with her parents, our boys and Dad. Followed a short while later by her brother and four sisters. With the visits to Annie's bed side in a process of rotation I manage to buy Dad a few pints of Guinness in the pub across the road.

He raises the first one aloft in honour of Annie, and takes a huge mouth full, almost half its measure, and with a dramatic lick of his lips he declares it's better than any mother's milk.

It's Tuesday 10th of April, when Annie links my arm and we walk to the car on Temple Street, late morning sun evaporates the damp from the pavements. With her head bandage removed it's difficult to see any sign of surgery through her thick wavy hair.

We walk slowly through the quiet street but I feel we are being watched, watched by an unseen crowd.

After two weeks at home Annie attends school again for half days. After two more weeks, she is in full attendance. Annie is scanned in Crumlin hospital every three months for the first year and a half after her surgery. With good results, that goes out to six months, in October 2014 they agree a scan once a year will suffice. In April 2017 she has her final follow-up scan, the results are all clear.

EPILOGUE

There she is now, that's Mommy. She's getting closer, her dark hair styled and big, her glasses slightly tinted and she's smiling at me in her striped blouse and black skirt. She looks good, she looks happy. She's speaking to me; her lips are moving but I can't hear anything. It's always the same, I can never hear her. I'm getting closer now, closer than any time before. I'm standing right in front of her but I'm taller than her now, she smiles her smile, so familiar but a smile I almost forgot. She holds her hands on my face as she talks in silence, I watch her mouth shape the words. "Keep on going, keep on going" she's mouthing, then a smile again. Now she's getting further away but she's not moving, it's me. I'm going backwards, she's getting smaller but she's smiling. I awaken in the dark, the red digits of the clock read 01:44. My heart is pounding wildly and I'm dribbling on my pillow. *That's the closest I've ever got to her*. I roll on my back; my heart is slowing to a normal pace. I shut my eyes and keep on going.

THE END

ACKNOWLEDGEMENTS

Thanks
For Tuition – Eileen Casey, John MacKenna,
Shauna Gilligan, Orla Murphy and Angela Keogh.
To Count on – Vinny Coyle & Mick Daly
For Everything – Niamh.